Casseroles

From Oven to Table Easy Everyday Casserole Recipes

Louise Davidson

Copyrights

All rights reserved © Louise Davidson and The Cookbook Publisher. No part of this publication or the information in it may be quoted from or reproduced in any form by means such as printing, scanning, photocopying, or otherwise without prior written permission of the copyright holder.

Disclaimer and Terms of Use

Effort has been made to ensure that the information in this book is accurate and complete. However, the author and the publisher do not warrant the accuracy of the information, text, and graphics contained within the book due to the rapidly changing nature of science, research, known and unknown facts, and internet. The author and the publisher do not hold any responsibility for errors, omissions, or contrary interpretation of the subject matter herein. This book is presented solely for motivational and informational purposes only.

ISBN: 978-1720375401

Printed in the United States

Contents

Introduction _____1

Breakfast _____7

Chicken and Turkey _____17

Beef _____41

Pork _____51

Vegetarian _____65

Desserts _____81

Recipe Index _____91

Also by Louise Davidson _____93

Appendix Cooking Conversion Charts _____95

Introduction

I love casseroles! They are easy to make. They can be as healthy or decadent as you want them to be. They will save you time and money and are perfect for meal prep or make-ahead meals. You can also freeze them for later use. You can bring them along for potlucks. Most of all, they are very comforting and satisfying. My family loves it because instead of being in the kitchen fixing dinner, I can enjoy quality time with all of them, knowing that their favorite meal will be ready to eat when we are. Finally, there is only one pot to clean! How easy is that? All you need are the right ingredients, a little time to prepare ahead of time, and a good baking dish.

Here are a few tips for making perfect casseroles.

Cut your ingredients evenly for even cooking

Big chunks of carrots with finely diced celery won't cook uniformly in a casserole. Keep in mind that unevenly chopped ingredients, especially vegetables, might become over- or undercooked.

Pre-cook some vegetables

Because different veggies have different cooking times, it's a good idea to partially cook some of your denser vegetables (like root vegetables – carrots, pumpkin, potatoes, parsnip, etc.) ahead of time. Blanch them for 1–2 minutes in boiling water before tossing them with the rest of the ingredients. You can also sauté onions to soften them and release their flavorful juices.

Save time with a flameproof casserole

Using a casserole dish that can go both on the stovetop and in the oven is a great time saver; you can brown or sauté the ingredients that need it and just use the same dish to bake the casserole. This means less time and less cleaning! A win-win option.

Avoid excess moisture

It's preferable to use fresh veggies and fruits whenever possible to avoid soggy casseroles. Since casserole ingredients cook in their own juice, and frozen veggies and fruits thaw in the casserole during cooking time, too much added liquid might make the casserole soggy and too wet. You can use frozen veggies as long as you thaw them beforehand and squeeze out the excess water.

Even some fresh vegetables carry a lot of moisture, so pre-cooking some might help prevent a soupy casserole. Fresh spinach and mushrooms are good examples. For spinach and similar veggies, squeezing out excess water is a must. For mushrooms, just browning them and getting rid of excess cooking juices will work well.

Using a sprinkle of flour or crumbled soda crackers can help absorb moisture in fruity casseroles.

The topping makes all the difference!

Using great toppings for the finishing touch on your casserole top layer will often make the difference between **an average casserole and an exquisite one!**

Use your imagination for extra flavors and textures. There are so many ingredients you can choose from, like bread crumbs, cereals, chips, bacon, butter crackers, all the cheeses you can shred or crumble, herbs, nuts, seeds, and so many more. Just keep in mind the flavor combination and the texture you want to get.

Cook your meats first

Most casserole recipes will ask you to brown your meat first to give it more flavor and keep it moist, just don't overcook it!

How to fill your casserole dish

There are basically two ways to assemble a casserole. The first is to mix all your ingredients together and toss them in the casserole. The second one is by layering your different ingredients for layers of flavors and textures. But the most important thing is not to over- or under-fill your dish. Usually fill the casserole three-quarters full, leaving enough space for it to bake properly. Under-filling your casserole dish might lead to overcooking, and over-filling might lead to a messy oven.

Casserole temperature matters!

It's always better to let your casserole come to room temperature before placing it in the oven to bake. This is especially true when you are using a frozen casserole. Baking it for a longer time might just overcook some ingredients and make a mushy mess. When the casserole is at room temperature the ingredients cook more evenly, rather than overcooking the edges and having cold spots in the middle.

Grate!

Don't want to spend time shopping for and pre-cooking some of your ingredients? Grate them instead! And then just squeeze out any excess moisture and add them (raw) to your casserole. This works particularly well for onions, garlic, cabbage, and carrots. It's even faster if you use a food processor.

Casserole are great for leftovers!

Have leftover chicken? With just a few other ingredients, it makes perfect casserole. It saves time. Made too much spaghetti sauce? Why not toss it with veggies and pasta, and make a pasta bake in no time. There are so many ways to use leftovers to make great casserole that will not only save time, but also avoid wasting food.

Use budget-friendly cuts of meat

Casserole are great for using budget-friendly tougher cuts of meat because they are cooked for longer periods of time and will become tender and delicious.

Fresh or dry herbs

Herbs give dishes great flavors. For casserole with a cooking time of more than 1 hour, use dry herbs rather than fresh, as fresh herbs have a tendency to lose their flavors when cooked for longer periods of time.

The kind of casserole dish can have an impact on the cooking time

In general, glass and metal baking dishes warm up faster than ceramic or stone casserole cookware, thus taking less time to cook. This will affect the cooking time by a few minutes in each case. Refer to the manufacturer for exact cooking time, depending on the material used.

To thicken sauces in your casserole

A quick and easy way to thicken the sauces from your casserole cooking juices is to dip meats, veggies or fruits lightly into flour before adding to the casserole.

Avoid mushy pasta casseroles!

Who likes overcooked, mushy pasta? No one of course! To avoid that, you just need to reduce the pasta package cooking time instructions by a few minutes (2–4 minutes). The pasta will continue cooking in the casserole in the oven.

Making casseroles ahead of time

Casseroles are the perfect dishes for make-ahead meals and frozen suppers. We all live fast and stressful lives and have no time to spare when it comes to mealtime. A great way to reduce our daily stress is to think ahead and plan our meals. When preparing a casserole, why not double up the recipe and make two – one you can serve during the next few days and the other to freeze and use later? In general, a prepared casserole can stay in the fridge up to 3–5 days, depending on the ingredients. To freeze, make sure to package it well and will keep fresh in the freezer, depending on the ingredients, up to 3 months.

Cover it!

A simple but effective way to cover a casserole dish (if it doesn't come with a lid), is to cover it up with aluminum foil. Make sure to lightly brush the foil with vegetable oil or butter or use cooking spray so food won't stick to it and ruin the casserole topping. Carefully remove the foil when it's time.

Make it crispy!

Your casserole will often require a crispy top. You have several options for that, which will be described in the directions of the recipes. In general, you can cook the casserole uncovered or you can remove the lid a few minutes before the cooking time is up. It can be a good idea, if you like a crispy topping, to add the topping ingredients after the casserole is cooked, and use the broiler for just a few minutes to make the top layer crispy. It takes only 5–15 minutes, depending on the ingredients.

Bringing your casserole along

A neat trick to keep a casserole warm while you bring it to a potluck or to eat somewhere else, is to simply place 3 or 4 kitchen towels in the bottom of a container, preferably a basket. Place the casserole on top and cover it with 3 or 4 more kitchen towels on top. It will keep the casserole warm for about 2 more hours.

Breakfast

Mushroom Hash Brown Morning Casserole

Serves: 6 - Prep. time: 10 minutes - Cooking time: 45 minutes

Ingredients:
2 medium potatoes
8 slices pork bacon
1 ½ cups onion, chopped
8 ounces shiitake mushrooms, sliced
2 cloves garlic, minced
¼ cup chicken stock
5 cups fresh baby spinach
2 tablespoons fresh parsley, chopped
Salt and pepper to taste
½ cup cheddar cheese, shredded, divided
½ cup milk
6 large eggs, lightly beaten
Cooking spray

Directions
1. Preheat the oven to 350°F and spray an 11x17" broiler-safe pan with cooking spray.
2. Peel and shred the potatoes. Line a colander with a clean kitchen towel and place the potatoes inside. Rinse well, and then gather the towel and squeeze out as much liquid from the potatoes as you can. Set aside, in the towel.
3. Cook the bacon in a large, non-stick skillet over medium-high heat, until crisp. Remove the bacon from the pan, chop it, and set it aside to cool.
4. Drain all but 1 tablespoon of the grease from the pan. Add the onion, mushrooms, and garlic, and sauté for 5 minutes, until they are softened and slightly browned.

5. Add the shredded potatoes and chicken stock. Cook for 5 minutes, stirring frequently.
6. Add the spinach and parsley, and season with salt and pepper. Cook briefly, until the spinach wilts.
7. Remove the skillet from the heat. Stir in the crumbled bacon and half the cheese.
8. Place the mushroom mixture in the prepared baking dish. (If you like, you can place it in the fridge at this point and continue with the next steps in the morning.)
9. Combine the milk and eggs and pour them over the vegetable mixture. Bake at 350° for 25 minutes.
10. In the final 5 minutes of baking, sprinkle the remaining cheese on top of the casserole. Turn on the broiler and cook until melted.

Nutrition (per serving)
Calories 278, Fat 10 g, Carbs 21 g, Protein 17 g, Sodium 618 mg

Pumpkin Spice Latte Quinoa Breakfast Casserole

Serves: 4 - Prep. time: 10 minutes - Cooking time: 1 hour

Ingredients
1 ½ cups warm water
¼ cup brewed coffee, hot or warm
2 tablespoons fresh or canned pumpkin purée
1 tablespoon maple syrup
1 teaspoon coconut oil, melted
¼ teaspoon pure vanilla extract
1 teaspoon pumpkin pie spice
½ cup dry quinoa

Topping
¼ cup chopped nuts
2 tablespoons oat flour
2 tablespoons honey
1 tablespoon almond flour
½ teaspoon cinnamon
Pinch salt
1 tablespoon coconut oil

Directions
1. Preheat the oven to 350°F.
2. Combine the water, coffee, pumpkin purée, maple syrup, coconut oil, vanilla, and pumpkin pie spice in a small casserole dish. Stir to combine.
3. Add the quinoa, and stir.
4. Cover and bake for 45–50 minutes, until most of the liquid is gone.
5. Meanwhile, combine the nuts, oat flour, honey, almond flour, cinnamon, and salt in a small bowl. Stir in the coconut oil, and set aside.

6. Once the casserole is done, remove it from the oven, and sprinkle with the topping. Return it to the oven, uncovered, and bake for another 10 minutes, until the topping browns.

Nutrition (per serving)
Calories 197, Fat 12 g, Carbs 20 g, Protein 3 g, Sodium 43 mg

Berry Cream Cheese French Toast Casserole

Serves: 4 - Prep. time: 10 minutes - Cooking time: 30 minutes

Ingredients
4-6 slices day-old French bread, cubed
4 eggs
¼ cup brown sugar
1 teaspoon vanilla extract
½ teaspoon cinnamon
Pinch allspice
1 ½ cups milk
½ cup blueberries
½ cup strawberries, sliced
2 ounces cream cheese, diced
Cooking spray
Optional toppings: maple syrup, whipped cream, icing sugar

Directions
1. Preheat the oven to 350°F. Lightly grease the bottom of an 8x8" baking dish.
2. Place the bread cubes in a large bowl.
3. In a medium bowl, whisk the eggs, brown sugar, vanilla, cinnamon, and allspice, and milk. Pour the custard mixture over the bread, and let it sit for 10 minutes, stirring once or twice.
4. Pour half the bread mixture into the bottom of the pan. Sprinkle half the berries and cream cheese on top. Top with remaining bread mixture, berries, and cheese.
5. Bake, covered, for 20 minutes. Uncover and bake 10 more minutes, or until the bread is golden brown and the casserole is set. Serve alone or with desired toppings.

Nutrition facts per serving
Calories 335, Fat 10 g, Carbs 50 g, Protein 13 g, Sodium 453 mg

Gobble Gobble Spinach and Mushroom Egg Bake

Serves: 8 - Prep. time: 10 minutes - Cooking time: 40 minutes

Ingredients
1 tablespoon olive oil
1 pound turkey sausage
1 medium onion, diced
1 clove garlic, minced
8 ounces frozen or fresh spinach
1 cup mushrooms, sliced
¼ cup carrot, grated
2 tablespoons fresh basil, chopped
Salt and pepper to taste
6 eggs
½ cup milk
3 ounces feta, crumbled

Directions
1. Preheat the oven to 400°F and spray a 9x13" casserole dish with cooking spray.
2. Heat 1 tablespoon of olive oil in a skillet and cook the sausage and onion for about 10 minutes, until the sausage is lightly browned and the onion is translucent.
3. Stir in the garlic, spinach, mushrooms, carrot, basil, salt, and pepper.
4. Place the sausage and vegetables in the prepared casserole dish.
5. In a mixing bowl, whisk the eggs and milk, and pour it over the sausage and veggie mixture. Top with feta.
6. Bake for 20 minutes, until the cheese is melted and the eggs are set.

Nutrition (per serving)
Calories 187, Fat 11 g, Carbs 4 g, Protein 17 g, Sodium 699 mg

Roasted Broccoli and Ham Breakfast Casserole

Serves: 12 - Prep. time: 10 minutes - Cooking time: 1 hour

Ingredients
1 head broccoli, florets only, cut into bite-sized pieces
2 tablespoons olive oil
Salt and pepper, to taste
1 cup cooked ham, cubed
½ cup Parmesan or Romana cheese, grated
1 red bell pepper, finely chopped
3 scallions, chopped
12 eggs
2 teaspoons herbes de Provence

Directions
1. Preheat the oven to 425°F and prepare a 9x13" casserole dish with cooking spray.
2. Toss the broccoli with olive oil, salt and pepper in a large bowl; transfer to a baking sheet.
3. Roast 25 minutes until browned, and remove the pan from the oven. Reduce the oven temperature to 375°F.
4. Gently combine the roasted broccoli, ham, Parmesan, red bell pepper, and scallions in a large bowl. Transfer the mixture to the prepared baking dish.
5. In a large mixing bowl, lightly beat the eggs, and stir in the herbes de Provence. Season with salt and pepper, and pour over the broccoli mixture.
6. Bake for 35 minutes, until the surface is lightly browned and the eggs are cooked through.

Nutrition (per serving)
Calories 249, Fat 17 g, Carbs 3 g, Protein 16 g, Sodium 361 mg

Overnight Sausage and Spiced Apple Breakfast Casserole

Serves: 12 - Prep. time: 15 minutes - Cooking time: 55–60 minutes

Ingredients
6 large, pre-cooked maple flavored pork breakfast sausages
10 eggs
3 cups milk
1 teaspoon vanilla
1 teaspoon salt
2 large apples, peeled and chopped
2 tablespoons brown sugar
1 teaspoon ground cinnamon
8 cups whole wheat bread, cubed
2 cups shredded cheddar cheese, divided

Directions
1. Slice the sausages into rounds and set them aside.
2. In a large bowl, whisk together the eggs, milk, vanilla, and salt until well blended.
3. In a separate bowl, mix the apples, sugar, and cinnamon together until well coated.
4. Grease a 9x13" baking dish, and place half the bread cubes in the bottom. Top with half the sausage, half the apple mixture, and half the cheese. Repeat the layers.
5. Pour the egg mixture over the casserole, making sure to evenly coat it all with the egg mixture.
6. Refrigerate overnight, to allow the bread to soak up a lot of the egg mixture.
7. In the morning, remove the casserole from the fridge and preheat the oven to 325°F.
8. Bake the casserole, uncovered, for 55–60 minutes, or until a knife inserted in the center comes out clean.

Nutrition facts per serving
Calories 314, Fat 18 g, Carbs 23 g, Protein 16 g, Sodium 161 mg

Overnight Sweet and Savory Breakfast Casserole

Serves:12 - Prep. time: 20 minutes - Cooking time: 45 minutes

Ingredients
1 teaspoon olive oil
12 ounces turkey breakfast sausage
2 cups milk
2 cups egg substitute
1 teaspoon dry mustard
Salt and pepper to taste
Pinch of red pepper flakes
3 large eggs
1 loaf white bread
1 cup cheddar cheese, shredded
Cooking spray
¼ cup green onion, chopped
Paprika, for sprinkling

Directions
1. Heat a large, non-stick skillet over medium-high heat, and heat the olive oil. Add the sausage to the pan, and cook for 5 minutes or until browned, stirring and crumbling the sausage.
2. Remove it from the heat and let it cool.
3. Combine the milk, egg substitute, mustard, salt, pepper, and red pepper flakes, and eggs in a large bowl, and whisk thoroughly.
4. Trim the crusts from bread and cut it into 1-inch cubes.
5. Add the bread cubes, sausage, and cheddar cheese to the custard mixture, stirring to combine. Pour it into a 9x13" baking dish, or a 3-quart casserole dish coated with cooking spray, spreading it evenly. Cover and refrigerate 8 hours or overnight.
6. In the morning (or when you're ready to cook) preheat the oven to 350°F.
7. Remove the casserole from the refrigerator and let it stand 30 minutes. Sprinkle with green onion and paprika.
8. Bake at 350° for 45 minutes or until set and lightly browned. Let stand 10 minutes.

Nutrition (per serving)
Calories 245, Fat 2 g, Carbs 20 g, Protein 9 g, Sodium 609 mg

Overnight Pumpkin French Toast

Serves: 10 - Prep. time: 15 minutes - Cooking time: 35–45 minutes

Ingredients
6–7 cups 1-inch bread cubes
7 large eggs
2 cups milk
1 teaspoon vanilla extract
2 teaspoons pumpkin pie spice
½ cup pumpkin purée
Cooking spray
4 tablespoons maple syrup, for topping
Optional: additional spice, nuts, raisins, shredded coconut, chopped apricots or dates

Directions
1. The night before, spray a 9x13" baking dish with cooking spray, and fill it with bread cubes.
2. In a large bowl, whisk the eggs, milk, vanilla, pumpkin purée, and pie spice until well combined. Pour it over the bread and gently push it down with a spoon until the bread is moistened or immersed. Cover, and refrigerate overnight.
3. In the morning, preheat the oven to 350°F.
4. Uncover the casserole and top with brown sugar, additional pumpkin pie spice, fruit, and nuts (optional).
5. Bake for 35–45 minutes, or until golden brown and set.
6. Drizzle with maple syrup and serve.

Nutrition (per serving, 1 slice)
Calories 122, Fat 4 g, Carbs 14 g, Protein 8 g, Sodium 145 mg

Chicken and Turkey

Chicken Tetrazzini

Serves: 8 - Prep. time: 30 minutes - Cooking time: 30 minutes

Ingredients
10 ounces dry linguine, cooked
2 tablespoons butter
¼ cup all-purpose flour
2 ½ cups chicken stock
1 ½ cups milk
½ cup grated Parmesan cheese, divided
1 ounce reduced-fat cream cheese
Salt and pepper to taste
4 teaspoons olive oil, divided
1 pound mushrooms, sliced
1 medium onion, chopped
5 cloves garlic, minced
1 teaspoon thyme
1 teaspoon marjoram
½ teaspoon tarragon
½ cup white wine
3 cups rotisserie chicken, shredded
1 cup frozen mixed vegetables
Cooking spray
2 cups bread crumbs
¼ cup fresh parsley, chopped

Directions
1. Preheat the oven to 375°F and prepare a 9x13" baking dish with cooking spray.
2. Melt the butter in a medium saucepan over medium heat. Stir in the flour and cook for 2 minutes, whisking constantly.
3. Gradually add the stock and milk and bring it to a boil. Reduce the heat, and simmer 5 minutes

4. Stir in half the Parmesan cheese, the cream cheese, salt, and pepper. Remove the pan from the heat and set it aside.
5. Heat a large skillet over medium-high heat. Add 1 tablespoon of olive oil to pan; swirl to coat. Add mushrooms and sauté 3 minutes, stirring occasionally. Add the onion, garlic, thyme, marjoram, and tarragon, and combine well.
6. Add the wine, stir, and cook for 1 minute.
7. Combine the cheese sauce, mushroom mixture, pasta, chicken, and vegetables. Spoon it into the prepared pan.
8. Combine the bread crumbs with the remaining Parmesan, and sprinkle it over the casserole.
9. Bake at 375°F for 30 minutes, or until browned and bubbly. Top with parsley.

Nutrition (per serving)
Calories 435, Fat 12 g, Carbs 45 g, Protein 33 g, Sodium 573 mg

Chicken Tamale Casserole

Serves: 8 - Prep. time: 20 minutes - Cooking time: 30 minutes

Ingredients
1 cup Mexican blend shredded cheese, divided
½ cup milk
1 egg
½ teaspoon ground cumin
½ teaspoon chili powder
⅛ teaspoon ground red pepper
1 clove garlic, minced
1 ½ cups cream-style corn
1 (8 ½ ounce) box corn muffin mix
1 (4 ounce) can chopped green chilies, drained
1 ½ cups red enchilada sauce (such as Old El Paso)
2 cups shredded rotisserie chicken
½ cup sour cream
½ cup cilantro, chopped
Cooking spray

Directions
1. Preheat the oven to 400°F and prepare a 9x13" baking dish with cooking spray.
2. In a large mixing bowl, combine ¼ cup of cheese with the milk, egg, cumin, chili powder, red pepper, garlic, corn, muffin mix, and green chilies. Stir just to combine.
3. Bake for 15 minutes, or until it is set. Pierce the entire surface liberally with a fork and pour the enchilada sauce over top.
4. Top with chicken, and sprinkle with the remaining ¾ cup cheese.
5. Bake for another 15 minutes, or until the cheese is melted.
6. Remove the casserole from the oven and let it stand 5 minutes.
7. Cut it into 8 pieces. Top each serving with 1 tablespoon of sour cream and garnish with cilantro.

Nutrition (per serving)
Calories 354, Fat 14 g, Carbs 36 g, Protein 19 g, Sodium 620 mg

Mom's Creamy Chicken and Broccoli Casserole

Serves: 6 - Prep. time: 10 minutes - Cooking time: 25 minutes

Ingredients
2 cups broccoli florets
1 tablespoon vegetable oil
1 cup onion, diced
1 pound mushrooms, sliced
2 cloves garlic, crushed and minced
1 stalk celery, diced
3 tablespoons all-purpose flour
1 ½ cups milk
1 teaspoon rubbed sage
3 cups skinless rotisserie chicken, chopped
½ cup plain fat-free Greek yogurt
¼ cup mayonnaise
Salt and pepper to taste
½ Swiss cheese, shredded
¼ cup Parmesan cheese, grated

Directions
1. Preheat the broiler.
2. In a small saucepan, boil 2 inches of water and steam the broccoli. Remove it from the heat promptly and drain the water.
3. Place a large, ovenproof skillet over medium-high heat. Heat the oil, and add the onion, mushrooms, garlic, and celery. Cook for 10 minutes, or until the mushrooms brown and the liquid evaporates, stirring occasionally.
4. Sprinkle the flour over the vegetables and stir for one minute. Add the milk and sage.
5. Bring it to a boil, and cook for 3 minutes, or until it is thick and bubbly.
6. Stir in the broccoli and chicken and cook to heat through.
7. Remove the pan from the heat. Add the yogurt, mayonnaise, salt, and pepper. Top with the cheeses and broil for 2 minutes.

Nutrition (per serving)
Calories 277, Fat 13 g, Carbs 15 g, Protein 29 g, Sodium 547 mg

King Ranch Chicken and Quinoa Casserole

Serves: 4 - Prep. time: 15 minutes - Cooking time: 40 minutes

Ingredients
2 cups cooked quinoa
1 tablespoon plus 2 teaspoons olive oil, divided
2 cups poblano peppers, chopped (about 3 medium)
1 ½ cups onion, chopped
1 tablespoon garlic, minced
2 tablespoons all-purpose flour
2 teaspoons ground cumin
1 teaspoon ancho chili powder
2 cups chicken stock
Salt and pepper to taste
1 (14 ½ ounce) can unsalted fire-roasted tomatoes
1 (4 ounce) can mild chopped green chilies
2 cups chicken breast, shredded
¾ cup cheddar cheese, shredded, divided
Cooking spray

Directions
1. Preheat the oven to 400°F and prepare an 8x8" baking dish with cooking spray.
2. Combine the cooked quinoa and 1 tablespoon of oil in a bowl. Spread the quinoa on a parchment-lined baking sheet and bake for 15 minutes.
3. Meanwhile, heat a large Dutch oven over medium-high heat. Add the remaining 2 teaspoons of oil. Add the poblano pepper, onion, and garlic; sauté 5 minutes.
4. Stir in the flour, cumin, and chili powder, and cook for 1 minute. Add the stock, salt and pepper, tomatoes, and chopped green chilies. Bring it to a boil, then reduce the heat, and simmer 5 minutes.
5. Remove the pan from the heat and stir in the chicken.

6. Pour half of the chicken mixture into the baking dish, and top with half of the quinoa and a quarter of the cheese.
7. Repeat the layers once with the remaining chicken mixture, remaining quinoa, and the rest of the cheese. Bake for 25 minutes.

Nutrition (per serving)
Calories 462, Fat 19 g, Carbs 45 g, Protein 32 g, Sodium 689 mg

Baked Chicken and Sweet Potato Enchilada

Serves: 9 - Prep. time: 30 minutes - Cooking time: 30–40 minutes

Ingredients
1 cup barbecue sauce of choice
1 ½ cups enchilada sauce
1 pound boneless skinless chicken breasts
2 teaspoons butter
½ small red onion, diced
2 cloves garlic, minced
2 medium sweet potatoes, cooked and diced
½ cup corn kernels
½ teaspoon cumin
½ teaspoon chili powder
9 (6 inch) corn tortillas
½ cup pepper jack cheese, shredded
½ cup mozzarella, shredded
½ cup cilantro, chopped
For topping: avocado and sour cream, if desired

Directions
1. Preheat the oven to 375°F and coat a 9x13" baking dish with cooking spray.
2. Whisk the barbecue and enchilada sauce together in a large bowl.
3. Arrange the chicken breasts in the baking pan, and drizzle ¼ cup of sauce on top. Bake for 20–25 minutes, or until juices run clear and chicken is no longer pink.
4. Remove the pan from the oven and allow the chicken to cool for a few minutes. Remove the chicken from the pan and shred it with forks. Set it aside, together with the cooking liquids.
5. Wipe out the pan and coat it with once more with cooking spray.
6. Meanwhile, melt the butter in a large skillet over medium-high heat. Add the onion and garlic and cook for a few minutes.

7. Add 1 cup of the enchilada sauce, the diced sweet potatoes, corn, cumin, and chili powder. Stir to combine, and then add it to the chicken mixture in the baking pan.
8. Place the remaining barbecue-enchilada sauce on a large plate. One at a time, dip three corn tortillas in the sauce (coating both sides) and arrange them in the baking dish, cutting one to fit, if necessary, to completely cover the bottom.
9. Place half the chicken and sweet potato mixture on top of the tortillas. Cover with ¼ cup of cheese, and about ¼ cup enchilada sauce. Repeat the layers once, and top with the remaining tortillas, sauce, and cheese.
10. Cover with foil and bake for 30–40 minutes, or until the enchiladas are warmed through and the cheese is completely melted. Cool a few minutes, garnish with cilantro, and then serve with sour cream and avocado if desired.

Nutrition (per serving)
Calories 276, Fat 8 g, Carbs 38 g, Protein 18 g, Sodium 745 mg

Creamy Chicken Quinoa and Broccoli Casserole

Serves: 6 - Prep. time: 10 minutes - Cooking time: 45–60 minutes

Ingredients
2 cups chicken broth
1 cup milk, divided
1 teaspoon poultry seasoning
½ cup all-purpose flour
2 cups water, divided
1 cup uncooked quinoa, rinsed
¼ cup cooked, crumbled bacon
1 pound boneless skinless chicken breasts
¼ cup mozzarella or Monterey jack cheese, shredded
3 cups fresh broccoli florets

Directions
1. Preheat the oven to 400°F and generously grease a 9x13" baking dish
2. Make the sauce. Bring the chicken broth and ½ cup milk to a low boil in a saucepan. Whisk the other ½ cup milk with the poultry seasoning and flour. Add the mixture to the boiling liquid and whisk until a creamy sauce forms.
3. In a large bowl, mix the sauce with one cup water, quinoa, and bacon, and stir to combine. Pour the mixture into the prepared baking dish. Slice the chicken breasts into thin strips and lay them over the quinoa mixture.
4. Bake, uncovered, for 30 minutes.
5. While the casserole is in the oven, place the broccoli in boiling water for 1 minute, until it turns bright green, and then run under cold water. Set it aside.
6. Remove the casserole from the oven and check the mixture by stirring it around in the pan. If it's not quite cooked, bake for an additional 10–15.

7. When the quinoa and chicken are cooked, and the sauce is thickened, add the broccoli and a little bit of water (up to one cup) until the consistency is creamy and smooth and you can stir it up easily in the pan.
8. Top with the cheese and bake for 5 minutes, or just long enough to melt the cheese.

Nutrition (per serving)
Calories 363, Fat 11 g, Carbs 31 g, Protein 34 g, Sodium 467 mg

Turkey Taco Mexican Lasagna

Serves: 8 - Prep. time: 15 minutes - Cooking time: 45 minutes

Ingredients
1 tablespoon olive oil
1 cup bell pepper, chopped
1 jalapeño pepper finely diced
1 cup sweet onion, chopped
2 cloves garlic, crushed and minced
1 ½ pounds leftover turkey meat
1 (15 ounce) can crushed tomatoes

Taco Spice Mix
1 ½ tablespoons cumin
1 ½ teaspoons paprika
1 ½ teaspoons salt
1 teaspoon chili powder
1 teaspoon cornstarch
½ teaspoon garlic powder
½ teaspoon black pepper
½ teaspoon red pepper flakes
¼ teaspoon cayenne pepper

1 cup frozen corn kernels
1 (15 ounce) can black beans, drained
2 cups shredded cheese (cheddar or Monterey Jack)
12 corn tortillas
Sour cream
½ cup green onions, chopped

Directions

1. Preheat the oven to 350°F and prepare a 9x13" baking dish with cooking spray.
2. Heat the oil in a large skillet over medium heat. Add the bell pepper, jalapeño, and onion. Sauté for 5 minutes.
3. Add the garlic and the cooked turkey to the skillet, and cook for 3–4 minutes, until the garlic is aromatic, and the turkey is warmed through.
4. Add the crushed tomatoes and simmer for a few minutes.
5. Combine the spice ingredients in a small bowl. Sprinkle the mixture into the skillet, stir, and let it simmer for another 5 minutes.
6. Start layering the Mexican lasagna with one-third of the turkey-tomato mixture.
7. Arrange 6 tortillas on that (cutting them if necessary), and cover with another third of the turkey mixture, half the corn, half the beans, and 1 cup of shredded cheese.
8. Repeat with the remaining tortillas, turkey, corn, beans, and cheese. Place aluminum foil over the baking dish and bake for 30 minutes.
9. Remove the aluminum foil and continue baking for 5 more minutes.
10. Let it sit for at least 10 minutes before serving. If you like, you can serve it with a dollop of sour cream, and some green onion on top.

Nutrition (per serving)
Calories 307, Fat 13 g, Carbs 25 g, Protein 23 g, Sodium 777 mg

Healthy Broccoli Chicken Casserole

Serves: 4 - Prep. time: 15 - Cooking time: 25 minutes

Ingredients
1 pound raw broccoli, chopped
1 pound cooked shredded chicken, cooked (about three large chicken breasts)
1 cup brown rice, cooked
1 (8 ounce) can sliced water chestnuts, drained
½ cup non-fat Greek yogurt
¼ cup milk
1 teaspoon garlic salt
½ teaspoon black pepper
¼ teaspoon thyme
¼ teaspoon paprika
¼ teaspoon rubbed sage
½ cup shredded mozzarella
1 cup shredded cheddar, divided
2 tablespoons panko breadcrumbs

Directions
1. Preheat the oven to 375°F and prepare a casserole dish with cooking spray.
2. Combine the broccoli, chicken, rice, and water chestnuts in a bowl.
3. In a separate bowl, mix together the Greek yogurt, milk, and seasonings. Once mixed completely, stir in the mozzarella and half the shredded cheddar.
4. Pour the yogurt mixture over the broccoli and chicken mixture. Mix well.
5. Spoon the casserole into the prepared casserole dish, and cover with the remining cheddar and the panko crumbs.
6. Bake for 25 minutes, until the broccoli is cooked through.

Nutrition (per serving)
Calories 449, Fat 17 g, Carbs 33 g, Protein 46 g, Sodium 601 mg

Tex-Mex Casserole

Serves: 4 - Prep. time: 15 minutes - Cooking time: 40 minutes

Ingredients
2 tablespoons vegetable oil
2 cups cooked chicken breasts, shredded meat
1 tablespoon taco spice mix (page 27)
1 (15 ounce) can black beans, rinsed and drained
1 (8 ¾ ounce) can sweet corn, drained
1 cup white rice, cooked
¼ cup salsa
Water as needed
1 cup shredded Mexican-style cheese
1 ½ cups crushed plain tortilla chips
½ cup cilantro, chopped

Directions
1. Preheat the oven to 350°F and prepare a 9x13 baking pan with cooking spray.
2. Place a large skillet over medium-high heat and heat the oil. Sauté the chicken until it is cooked through.
3. Add the taco seasoning, beans, corn, rice, salsa, and a little water to prevent it from drying out. Cover the skillet and simmer over medium low-heat for 10 minutes.
4. Transfer the chicken mixture to the baking dish. Top with half the cheese and all the crushed tortilla chips.
5. Bake for 15 minutes. Add the remaining cheese and bake until it is melted and bubbly. Garnish with cilantro before serving.

Nutrition (per serving)
Calories 531, Fat 21 g, Carbs 53 g, Protein 36 g, Sodium 1430 mg

Chicken Mushroom and Potato Bake

Serves: 4–5 - Prep. time: 20 minutes - Cooking time: 1 ½ hours

Ingredients
6 strips bacon, chopped
1 small onion, diced
3 pounds potatoes, peeled and sliced ⅛" thick
8 ounces chicken breast, cut in 1-inch pieces
8 ounces mushrooms, quartered
Salt and pepper, to taste
Onion powder
⅓ cup cheddar, shredded
½ cup chicken stock
¼ cup cream
¼ cup chopped green onion
½ cup Italian parsley, chopped, to garnish

Directions
1. Preheat the oven to 450°F and grease a casserole dish with cooking spray.
2. Heat a skillet over medium heat and fry the bacon until crisp. Drain all but 2 tablespoons of the grease.
3. Add the onion to the bacon and continue cooking until the onion is cooked. Spoon the onion and garlic from the fat and set it aside.
4. Turn the heat to high and add the quartered mushrooms to the bacon fat and brown them over high heat, stirring frequently. Remove the skillet from the heat.
5. Season the sliced potatoes with the salt, pepper, and onion powder and toss to coat the slices evenly.
6. Season the chicken with salt, pepper, and onion powder as well.
7. Layer the ingredients: the chicken, half the bacon and onion mixture, a bit of cheese, mushrooms, bacon mixture, a little more cheese, and then arrange the potatoes on the top.
8. Mix the chicken stock and cream together and pour it on top. Cover the baking dish with foil or a lid.

9. Bake for 15 minutes, then reduce the heat to 350°F and bake for another 40 minutes. Remove the foil or the lid and cook for additional 15 minutes, or until the top is golden brown and the potatoes are tender.
10. Sprinkle the last of the cheese on top and add the green onion and parsley.

Nutrition (per serving)
Calories 308, Fat 12 g, Carbs 31 g, Protein 18 g, Sodium 287 mg

Enchiladas Supreme

Serves: 4-6 - Prep. time: 20 minutes - Cooking time: 40 minutes

Ingredients
1 (10.75 ounce) can condensed cream of chicken soup
1 ¼ cups sour cream
½ teaspoon chili powder
½ teaspoon cumin
1 tablespoon butter
1 small onion, chopped
1 clove garlic, minced
2 pounds rotisserie chicken, shredded
1 (4 ounce) can chopped green chilies, drained
2 tablespoons taco spice mix (page 27)
1 bunch green onions, chopped, divided
1 cup water
1 teaspoon lemon juice
1 teaspoon garlic powder
5 (12 inch) flour tortillas
3 cups cheddar cheese, shredded, divided
1 ½ cups enchilada sauce
½ cup cilantro, chopped

Directions
1. Preheat the oven to 350°F. Grease a 9x13" baking dish with cooking spray.
2. Combine the cream of chicken soup, sour cream, chili powder, and cumin in a saucepan. Bring it to a simmer over low heat, stirring occasionally, then turn off the heat and cover the pot.
3. Melt the butter in a skillet over medium heat. Stir in the onion and garlic, and cook until the onion has softened, about 5 minutes.
4. Add the shredded chicken, chopped green chilies, taco seasoning, half of the green onion, and water. Simmer for 10 minutes.
5. Stir in the lemon juice and garlic powder and stir to combine.

6. Mix 1 cup of the soup mixture into the skillet with the chicken mixture. Spread the remaining soup mixture in the baking dish.
7. Divide the chicken mixture among the tortillas and sprinkle a generous tablespoon of cheddar over the chicken filling before folding the tortillas. (Half will be left for topping.)
8. Arrange the tortillas seam-side down on the sauce in the prepared baking pan.
9. Pour the enchilada sauce evenly over the enchiladas. Cover with the remaining cheddar cheese. Sprinkle the reserved chopped green onions.
10. Bake until the filling is heated through and the cheese is melted and bubbling, about 25 minutes.
11. Garnish with cilantro and serve.

Nutrition (per serving)
Calories 709, Fat 36 g, Carbs 52 g, Protein 42 g, Sodium 1764 mg

Turkey Sausage Potato Bake

Serves: 4 - Prep. time: 20 minutes - Cooking time: 45 minutes

Ingredients
2 (4 ounce) hot turkey Italian sausage links, casings removed
1 tablespoon butter
2 cups onion, chopped
4 ounces white mushrooms, sliced
2 pounds red potatoes, coarsely chopped
1 teaspoon salt
1 teaspoon pepper
½ teaspoon thyme
¼ teaspoon paprika
½ cup chicken broth
½ cup Swiss cheese, shredded
½ cup Parmesan cheese, shredded
¼ cup fresh parsley, chopped

Directions
1. Preheat the oven to 400°F, and spray a 3-quart baking dish with cooking spray
2. Heat a large, non-stick skillet over medium-high heat. Add the sausage, and sauté for 5 minutes or until browned, stirring to crumble.
3. Remove the sausage to a plate and drain it on paper towel.
4. Melt the butter in the pan. Add the onion and cook for 4 minutes, stirring occasionally. Add the mushrooms and sauté for 6 minutes, stirring occasionally.
5. Add the potatoes, salt, pepper, thyme, and paprika. Cook until browned, about 5 minutes.
6. Stir in the sausage and broth.
7. Spoon the potato mixture into the prepared baking dish, and top with cheese.
8. Cover, and bake for 30 minutes. Uncover, and bake an additional 15 minutes or until golden. Sprinkle with fresh parsley and serve.

Nutrition (per serving)
Calories 358, Fat 13 g, Carbs 40 g, Protein 19 g, Sodium 619 mg

Dreamy Creamy Enchiladas

Serves: 6 - Prep. time: 15 minutes - Cooking time: 15 minutes

Ingredients
2 cups cooked chicken, shredded
1 cup sour cream
¼ teaspoon salt
¼ teaspoon black pepper
2 tablespoons chives, minced
½ cup vegetable oil for frying
12 (5 inch) corn tortillas
1 (4 ounce) can chopped green chilies, drained
2 cups shredded Monterey Jack cheese

Directions
1. Preheat the oven to 400°F and grease a 9x13" baking dish with cooking spray. Set out a plate with paper towel on it, to work on.
2. Combine the chicken, sour cream, salt, pepper, and chives in a bowl and set it aside.
3. Heat the oil in a skillet over medium-high heat. Dip the corn tortillas into the hot oil one at a time until softened, about 10 seconds each. Quickly set them on the paper-lined plate and spoon a heaping tablespoon of chicken mixture onto each one. Spread it down the center and roll the tortilla into a cylinder.
4. Place the tortillas seam-side down into the prepared baking dish. When all the tortillas are filled and rolled, sprinkle the green chilies over and top with the shredded Monterey Jack cheese.
5. Bake until the cheese has melted and the enchiladas are hot, 12–15 minutes.

Nutrition (per serving)
Calories 434, Fat 26 g, Carbs 24 g, Protein 26 g, Sodium 540 mg

Zucchini Chicken Bake

Serves: 4 - Prep. time: 20 minutes - Cooking time: 30 minutes

Ingredients
1 egg
1 tablespoon water
Salt and pepper to taste
1 cup dry bread crumbs, divided
4 tablespoons olive oil, divided
4 skinless, boneless chicken breast halves
5 zucchinis, sliced
1 small onion, minced
3 cloves garlic, minced
4 tomatoes, sliced
1 cup mozzarella cheese, shredded, divided
2 teaspoons fresh basil, chopped

Directions
1. Preheat the oven to 400°F. Lightly grease a 9x13" baking dish.
2. Beat the egg, water, salt, and pepper in a shallow bowl. Set 2 tablespoons of bread crumbs aside and pour the remaining bread crumbs into a large resealable plastic bag.
3. Dip the chicken pieces in the egg mixture, and then place them in the bag and shake to coat.
4. Heat 2 tablespoons of the olive oil in a large skillet over medium. Cook the chicken until browned, 2 to 3 minutes per side. Remove the chicken from the pan.
5. Add the remaining 2 tablespoons of oil to the skillet. Add the zucchini, onion, and garlic, and cook over medium heat until the zucchini is slightly tender and the onion is softened, about 2 minutes. Transfer the vegetables to the prepared baking dish.
6. Sprinkle the reserved bread crumbs over the zucchini. Top with tomato slices, three-quarters of the mozzarella cheese, and basil. Place the chicken on top.
7. Cover with aluminum foil and bake until the chicken is no longer pink in the center, about 25 minutes.
8. Uncover, and sprinkle with the remaining mozzarella cheese. Bake until the cheese is melted, about 5 minutes.

Nutrition (per serving)
Calories 506, Fat 24 g, Carbs 34 g, Protein 40 g, Sodium 768 mg

Easy Tex-Mex Chicken

Serves: 4 - Prep. time: 15 minutes - Cooking time: 20 minutes

Ingredients
4 boneless, skinless chicken breasts
1 tablespoon olive oil
1 clove garlic, minced
Salt and pepper to taste
½ teaspoon ground cumin
½ teaspoon chili powder
Pinch red pepper flakes
1 cup salsa
1 cup shredded cheddar cheese
Cooked white rice, for serving

Directions
1. Preheat the oven to 375°F and grease an 8x8" baking pan with cooking spray.
2. Heat a skillet over medium heat and warm the oil. Rub the chicken pieces with garlic, salt, pepper, cumin, chili powder, and red pepper flakes.
3. Cook the chicken until it is brown on both sides and no longer pink in the middle, about 10 minutes.
4. Place the chicken in the baking dish. Top with salsa and cheese and bake until the cheese is bubbly and starts to brown, about 20 minutes.
5. Serve with rice, if desired.

Nutrition (per serving)
Calories 286, Fat 15 g, Carbs 5 g, Protein 35 g, Sodium 641 mg

Southern Chicken and Biscuit Bake

Serves: 6 - Prep. time: 20 minutes - Cooking time: 50 minutes

Ingredients
¼ cup butter
2 cloves garlic, minced
1 small onion, chopped
2 stalks celery, chopped
¼ cup baby carrots, chopped
½ cup all-purpose flour
1 teaspoon white sugar
1 teaspoon salt
1 teaspoon dried marjoram
½ teaspoon ground black pepper
4 cups chicken broth
1 cup frozen peas, thawed
4 cups diced, cooked chicken meat
2 cups buttermilk baking mix
2 teaspoons dried basil
⅔ cup milk

Directions
1. Preheat the oven to 350°F and coat a 9x13" baking dish with cooking spray.
2. In a skillet, melt the butter over medium-high heat. Cook and stir in the garlic, onion, celery, and carrots until they are tender. Mix in the flour, sugar, salt, marjoram, and pepper.
3. Stir in the broth and bring the mixture to a boil. Stirring constantly, boil for 1 minute. Reduce the heat and stir in the peas and the chicken. Simmer 5 minutes, then transfer the mixture to the prepared baking dish.
4. In a medium bowl, combine the baking mix and basil. Stir in the milk to form a dough. Divide the dough into 8 balls. On floured wax paper, use the palm of your hand to flatten each ball of dough into a circular shape and place them on top of the chicken mixture.
5. Bake for 30 minutes. Cover with foil and bake for 10 more minutes. To serve, spoon the chicken mixture over the biscuits.

Nutrition (per serving)
Calories 450, Fat 13 g, Carbs 48 g, Protein 33 g, Sodium 205 mg

Beef

Quick Pastitsio

Serves: 6 - Prep. time: 10 minutes - Cooking time: 25 minutes

Ingredients
8 ounces uncooked penne
1 tablespoon olive oil
1 pound ground beef
1 large onion, diced
5 cloves garlic, minced
1 teaspoon salt
½ teaspoon black pepper
¼ teaspoon dried oregano
1 tablespoon all-purpose flour
2 cups milk
1 (14 ½ ounce) can diced tomatoes, drained
8 ounces reduced fat cream cheese
½ cup mozzarella cheese, shredded
2 tablespoons chopped fresh flat-leaf parsley

Directions
1. Preheat the broiler and coat a 9x13" baking pan with cooking spray.
2. Cook the pasta according to the package directions. Drain well.
3. Meanwhile, heat a large skillet over medium-high heat. Warm the olive oil and add the beef to the pan. Sauté for 5 minutes or until browned, stirring to crumble. Drain any excess grease.
4. Add the onion and sauté until tender, stirring occasionally. Add the garlic and cook one more 1 minute, stirring constantly.
5. Season the mixture with salt, pepper, and oregano. Sprinkle the flour over the meat and cook for 1 minute, stirring frequently.
6. Stir in the milk, tomatoes, and cream cheese until smooth. Bring the mixture to a simmer. Cook until it is heated through and stir in the pasta.

7. Spoon the pasta mixture into the baking dish and sprinkle it with the mozzarella.
8. Broil for 4 minutes or until golden. Sprinkle with parsley.

Nutrition (per serving)
Calories 431, Fat 16 g, Carbs 42 g, Protein 28 g, Sodium 679 mg

Unstuffed Cabbage Casserole

Serves: 6 - Prep. time: 15 minutes - Cooking time: 1 hour

Ingredients
2 pounds cabbage, roughly chopped
1 pound ground beef
2 tablespoons butter
1 large onion, chopped
4 cloves garlic, minced
½ cup tomato paste
½ cup tomatoes, diced
1 cup rice, rinsed
1 ½ teaspoons salt
1 teaspoon black pepper
1 teaspoon Italian seasoning
1 bunch parsley, chopped
3/4 cup water
2 cans condensed tomato soup

Directions
1. Blanch the cabbage in boiling water for 5–10 minutes, until tender. Drain, cover, and set aside.
2. Meanwhile, cook the ground beef over medium heat, and drain any excess fat.
3. Push the beef to the side, and add the butter, onion, and garlic. Stir in the vegetables and cook for 5–10 minutes, covered.
4. Add the tomato paste, chopped tomatoes, rice, salt, pepper, Italian seasoning, parsley, and water. Stir well.
5. Cover, and cook on medium-low until the water is absorbed and the rice is cooked, about 15 minutes.
6. Preheat the oven to 350°F and coat a 3-quart casserole dish with cooking spray.
7. Stir in the cabbage and spoon the mixture into the baking dish. Spread the condensed tomato soup on top.
8. Bake for 30 minutes.

Nutrition (per serving)
Calories 466, Fat 21 g, Carbs 52 g, Protein 20 g, Sodium 1130 mg

Superfood Taco Casserole

Serves: 6 - Prep. time: 20 minutes - Cooking time: 1 hour

Ingredients
1 tablespoon vegetable oil
1 pound ground beef
1 cup chicken stock
1 cup uncooked quinoa, rinsed
1 (28 ounce) can of diced tomatoes
2 tablespoons taco spice mix (page 27)
1 red bell pepper, chopped
3 green onions (white and greens only), chopped
1 cup corn kernels
1 cup canned black beans, rinsed and drained
3 cups kale, chopped and stemmed
1 cup cheddar or Monterey Jack cheese, shredded

Directions
1. Preheat the oven to 350°F and coat a 9x13" baking dish with cooking spray.
2. Heat the vegetable oil in a skillet and cook the ground beef. Drain any excess grease.
3. Pour the chicken stock into the baking dish and stir in the dry quinoa.
4. In a large bowl, combine the tomatoes with the spices, and pour half of this mixture over the quinoa.
5. Top with the ground beef, bell pepper, green onions, corn, black beans, and kale.
6. Pour the remaining tomatoes on top, and sprinkle with cheese.
7. Cover the dish with foil, and bake for 45 minutes, then remove the foil and continue baking for 15 minutes longer.

Nutrition (per serving)
Calories 448, Fat 21 g, Carbs 47 g, Protein 28 g, Sodium 769 mg

Beefy Tots Casserole

Serves: 8 - Prep. time: 15 minutes - Cooking time: 50 minutes

Ingredients
1 (32 ounce) bag frozen bite-size potato nuggets (such as Tater Tots®), divided
1 pound ground beef
1 large onion, chopped
1 tablespoon Worcestershire sauce
1 teaspoon Montreal-style steak seasoning
1 teaspoon garlic powder
1 (10 ¾ ounce) can condensed cream of mushroom soup
½ cup milk
1 ½ cups cheddar cheese, shredded, divided
½ cup cilantro, for garnishing

Directions
1. Preheat the oven to 350°F and coat a 9x13" casserole dish with cooking spray.
2. Spread 20 potato nuggets in the casserole dish, and bake until warmed through, about 10 minutes.
3. Meanwhile, heat a large skillet over medium-high heat. Cook and stir the beef and onion until the beef is completely browned, 5–7 minutes. Drain any excess grease.
4. Season the beef mixture with the Worcestershire sauce, steak seasoning, and garlic powder.
5. Combine the cream of mushroom soup, milk, 1/2 cup Cheddar cheese, and 1 teaspoon Worcestershire sauce together in a bowl.
6. Using a fork or potato masher, crush the warmed potato nuggets in the casserole dish to cover the bottom completely. Spread the ground beef mixture over the mashed potato nuggets. Pour the soup mixture evenly over the beef layer. Top with remaining potato nuggets and sprinkle the remaining cheddar cheese evenly over the top.
7. Bake until the casserole is bubbly and the potatoes are golden brown, 30–40 minutes. Sprinkle with cilantro and serve.

Nutrition (per serving)
Calories 477, Fat 27 g, Carbs 38 g, Protein 25 g, Sodium 1219 mg

Spaghetti Squash Beef and Bubble

Serves: 6 - Prep. time: 15 minutes - Cooking time: 1 hour, 15 minutes

Ingredients
1 spaghetti squash, halved and seeded
1 pound ground beef
½ cup diced green bell pepper
½ cup diced red bell pepper
¼ cup diced red onion
2 cloves garlic, minced
1 (14 ½ ounce) can Italian-style diced tomatoes, drained
½ cup prepared salsa
1 ½ teaspoons Italian seasoning
Salt and pepper to taste
2 ¼ cups cheddar cheese, shredded, divided

Directions
1. Preheat the oven to 375°F.
2. Place the squash on a baking sheet, and bake it for 40 minutes, or until tender. Remove it from the heat, cool, and shred the pulp with a fork.
3. Reduce the oven temperature to 350°F. Lightly grease a casserole dish.
4. In a skillet over medium heat, cook the ground beef. Drain any excess grease, and mix in the green pepper, red pepper, red onion, and garlic. Continue to cook and stir until the vegetables are tender.
5. Mix the shredded squash, tomatoes, and salsa into the skillet, and season with Italian seasoning, salt, and pepper. Cook and stir until heated through.
6. Remove the skillet from the heat, and mix in 2 cups of the cheese, until melted. Transfer to the prepared casserole dish.
7. Bake for 25 minutes, and then sprinkle with the remaining cheese, and continue baking 5 minutes, until the cheese is melted.

Nutrition (per serving)
Calories 399, Fat 26 g, Carbs 13 g, Protein 27 g, Sodium 590 mg

Easy Beef Casserole

Serves: 6 - Prep. time: 5 minutes - Cooking time: 40 minutes

Ingredients
3 ½ cups farfalle (bow tie) pasta, uncooked
1 pound ground beef
2 cloves garlic, minced
1 (15 ounce) can tomato sauce
1 cup sour cream
1 teaspoon dried thyme
½ cup green olives, chopped
½ cup parsley, chopped
1 cup shredded mozzarella cheese

Directions
1. Preheat the oven to 350°F and prepare a 2-quart casserole dish with cooking spray.
2. Bring a pot of water to a boil. Add the pasta, and cook until tender, about 8 minutes.
3. Crumble the ground beef into a skillet and cook over medium-high heat. Drain any excess grease, and stir in the garlic, tomato sauce, sour cream, and thyme.
4. Place the cooked pasta in the casserole dish and spoon the ground beef mixture over it. Sprinkle on the olives and the parsley
5. Top with shredded cheese, and bake for 30 minutes, until heated through and lightly browned on the top.

Nutrition (per serving)
Calories 386, Fat 22 g, Carbs 24 g, Protein 24 g, Sodium 704 mg

Ravioli Twist

Serves: 8 - Prep. time: 10 minutes - Cooking time: 50 minutes

Ingredients
16 ounces dry pasta
1 (10 ounce) package frozen, chopped spinach
1 pound lean ground beef
1 small chopped onion, diced
1 clove garlic, minced
1 (8 ounce) can tomato sauce
1 (6 ounce) can tomato paste
2 cups pasta sauce
½ cup bread crumbs
2 eggs, beaten
¼ cup chicken or beef broth
1 cup mozzarella cheese, shredded

Directions
1. Preheat the oven to 350°F and prepare a 9x13" baking dish with cooking spray.
2. In a medium pot, cook the pasta in boiling salted water until al dente. Drain well.
3. Cook the spinach according to the package directions.
4. Meanwhile, brown the ground beef in a large skillet over medium heat, and drain the fat. Add the chopped onion, and minced garlic. Stir in the tomato sauce, tomato paste, and pasta sauce. Simmer for 10 minutes.
5. Combine the cooked spinach, cooked pasta, bread crumbs, eggs, broth or water, and shredded cheese.
6. Spread the spinach mixture evenly in the baking dish. Top with the meat mixture. Cover with aluminum foil.
7. Bake for 30 minutes and serve.

Nutrition (per serving)
Calories 526, Fat 25 g, Carbs 52 g, Protein 26 g, Sodium 779 mg

Beef Stew Bake

Serves: 5 - Prep. time: 20 minutes - Cooking time: 3–3 ½ hours

Ingredients
3 cups water
1 tablespoon vegetable oil
1 tablespoon butter
2 celery ribs, roughly chopped
1 large onion, roughly chopped
3 large carrots, roughly chopped
2 small potatoes, peeled and chopped
3 cloves garlic, roughly chopped
3 bay leaves
3 sprigs thyme, divided
2 tablespoons all-purpose flour
2 tablespoons tomato purée
2 tablespoons Worcestershire sauce
2 beef stock cubes, crumbled
2 pounds stewing beef, in large chunks

Directions
1. Heat the oven to 350°F, and boil 3 cups of water.
2. In a Dutch oven, warm the vegetable oil and butter together. Cook the celery, onion, carrots, potatoes, garlic, bay leaves and 1 thyme sprig. Cook for 10 minutes, stirring occasionally.
3. Stir in the flour, followed by the tomato purée, Worcestershire sauce, beef stock cubes, and the remaining thyme sprigs.
4. Gradually stir in the hot water, and then add the beef and bring the mixture to a gentle simmer.
5. Cover and bake for 2 ½ hours, then uncover and cook for ½ to 1 hour more, until the meat is really tender and the sauce is thickened.
6. Remove the thyme twigs and bay leaves before serving.

Nutrition (per serving)
Calories 538, Fat 33 g, Carbs 16 g, Protein 36 g, Sodium 1600 mg

Beef Goulash

Serves: 6 - Prep. time: 15 minutes - Cooking time: 2 hours

Ingredients
3 tablespoons butter, divided
2 pounds beef chuck, cut into chunks
2 tablespoons all-purpose flour
1 large onion, thinly sliced
2 cloves garlic, minced
½ green pepper, deseeded and thinly sliced
½ red pepper, deseeded and thinly sliced
2 tablespoons tomato paste
2 tablespoons paprika (good quality is essential)
1 ½ cups canned tomatoes, drained
⅓ cup dry white wine
1 ½ cups beef stock
Salt and pepper to taste
⅔ cup sour cream
2 tablespoons parsley, chopped
Mashed potatoes, for serving

Directions
1. Preheat the oven to 350°F.
2. Heat 2 tablespoons of butter in a Dutch oven. Sprinkle the beef with the flour and brown it well, working in batches. Set the browned meat aside.
3. Add the remaining butter to the pot, and cook the onion, garlic, green pepper and red pepper until they are softened, about 5 minutes.
4. Return the beef to the pot and stir in the tomato paste and paprika. Cook, stirring, for 2 minutes.
5. Add the tomatoes, white wine and beef stock. Cover and bake for 1 ½–2 hours, until the meat is tender.
6. Season with salt and freshly ground pepper.
7. Stir in the sour cream and garnish with parsley. Serve with potatoes, if desired.

Nutrition (per serving)
Calories 386, Fat 15 g, Carbs 34 g, Protein 28 g, Sodium 1466 mg

Pork

Bacon with Roasted Butternut Squash Pasta

Serves: 4-6 - Prep. time: 15 minutes - Cooking time: 1 hour

Ingredients
1 teaspoon salt, divided
½ teaspoon dried rosemary
Salt and pepper to taste
3 cups butternut squash, peeled and cut in 1-inch cubes
½ pound hickory-smoked bacon slices (uncooked)
½ cup shallots, thinly sliced
8 ounces small penne or macaroni pasta (uncooked)
¼ cup all-purpose flour
2 cups milk
¾ cup sharp provolone cheese, shredded
⅓ cup fresh Parmesan cheese, grated

Directions
1. Preheat the oven to 425°F and prepare a 2-quart baking dish with cooking spray.
2. Combine ¼ teaspoon salt with the rosemary and pepper. Place the squash on a foil-lined baking sheet coated with cooking spray. Sprinkle it with the salt mixture.
3. Bake for 45 minutes, or until tender and lightly browned. Increase the oven temperature to 450°F.
4. Meanwhile, cook the bacon in a large non-stick skillet over medium heat until crisp. Remove the bacon from the pan, reserving 1 tablespoon of the fat. Crumble the bacon and set it aside.
5. Increase the heat to medium-high. Add the shallots to the pan and cook a few minutes, until tender. Combine the squash mixture, bacon, and shallots, and set aside.
6. Cook the pasta according to the package directions.

7. Combine the flour and the remaining salt in a Dutch oven over medium-high heat. Gradually add the milk, stirring constantly with a whisk, and bring it to a boil. Cook for 1 minute or until slightly thickened and remove it from the heat.
8. Add the provolone and stir until the cheese melts. Add the pasta to the cheese sauce and combine.
9. Spoon the pasta mixture into the baking dish, and top with the squash mixture. Sprinkle evenly with Parmesan cheese.
10. Bake for 10 minutes, or until the cheese melts and begins to brown.

Nutrition (per serving)
Calories 494, Fat 21 g, Carbs 56 g, Protein 21 g, Sodium 1006 mg

Broccoli Sausage Quinoa Casserole

Serves: 12 - Prep. time: 20 minutes - Cooking time: 40 minutes

Ingredients
2 ½ cups water
2 cups uncooked quinoa, rinsed and drained
¼ cup butter, divided
1 small onion, diced
½ cup carrot, peeled and diced
4 (4 ounce) links sweet chicken Italian sausage, casings removed
¼ cup all-purpose flour
3 cloves garlic, minced
2 cups whole milk
2 cups unsalted chicken stock
6 cups fresh broccoli florets, chopped
1 tablespoon fresh thyme, divided
Salt and pepper to taste
¼ teaspoon crushed red pepper
½ cup whole wheat breadcrumbs
1 cup cheddar cheese, shredded

Directions
1. Preheat the oven to 400°F and prepare two 8x8" baking pans with cooking spray.
2. Boil the water in a medium saucepan and add the quinoa. Reduce the heat, cover, and simmer 12–14 minutes, or until the liquid is absorbed. Remove the pot from the heat and let it stand 5 minutes.
3. Heat a large Dutch oven over medium-high heat. Add 1 tablespoon of butter and swirl until it's melted.
4. Add the onion, carrot, and sausage. Cook 7 minutes, stirring to crumble the sausage. Remove the sausage mixture to a bowl, and cover.
5. Add flour, remaining butter, and garlic to the drippings in pan and cook 2 minutes, stirring frequently. Add the milk and stock and bring it to a boil.

6. Cook 2 minutes, whisking constantly. Reduce the heat to medium. Stir in the broccoli, 2 teaspoons thyme, salt, black pepper, and red pepper flakes. Cover and cook 2 minutes.
7. Stir in the quinoa and the sausage mixture.
8. Divide the quinoa mixture between the baking dishes.
9. In a mixing bowl, combine the panko with the remaining 1 teaspoon thyme, and season with salt and pepper. Stir in the cheddar and divide the mixture over the two pans.
10. Bake for 20 minutes, or until browned.

Nutrition (per serving)
Calories 296, Fat 13 g, Carbs 28 g, Protein 17 g, Sodium 399 mg

Creamy Cauliflower with Bacon

Serves: 4–6 - Prep. time: 10 minutes - Cooking time: 30 minutes

Ingredients
1 large head cauliflower
4–6 strips bacon
1 cup sour cream
½ cup shredded Monterey jack cheese, divided
Salt and pepper to taste

Directions
1. Preheat the oven to 350°F, and lightly grease a casserole dish with olive oil spray.
2. Fill a large pot with 1–2" of water and bring it to a boil. Cut the cauliflower into bite-sized pieces and add it to the boiling water, cover, and reduce the heat to low.
3. Steam the cauliflower until it is fork tender and drain well.
4. Meanwhile, cook the bacon until crisp. Remove the bacon and crumble, reserving the bacon grease.
5. Pour the cauliflower into the casserole dish and drizzle the bacon grease on top. Stir in the sour cream, half the shredded cheese, and half the crumbled bacon. Stir until well coated.
6. Top with the remaining cheese and bacon, and bake for 15–20 minutes, or until the cheese is melted.

Nutrition (per serving)
Calories 213, Fat 14 g, Carbs 10 g, Protein 11 g, Sodium 558 mg

Pork and Cabbage

Serves: 6 - Prep. time: 15 minutes - Cooking time: 1 hour

Ingredients
4 slices bacon
6 country-style pork ribs
Salt and pepper to taste
5 cups cabbage, shredded
1 medium onion, chopped
1 large apple, chopped
3 carrots, julienned
¾ cup apple cider (or juice)
1 teaspoon celery seed

Directions
1. Preheat the oven to 350°F and grease a 9x13" casserole dish.
2. In a medium skillet, cook the bacon. Remove it from the drippings and crumble it in a bowl.
3. Season the ribs with salt and pepper and cook them in the bacon grease for 3-4 minutes on high heat, turning once. Remove them to the casserole dish.
4. Cook the cabbage and onion until softened in the bacon grease.
5. Mix in the apple, carrots, apple cider, and celery seed. Spoon this mixture over top of the pork, and sprinkle with bacon.
6. Cover with foil and bake 30–45 minutes.

Nutrition (per serving)
Calories 322, Fat 18 g, Carbs 13 g, Protein 27 g, Sodium 349.7 mg

Quick Shepherd's Pie

Serves: 6 - Prep. time: 10 minutes - Cooking time: 25 minutes

Ingredients
1 (24 ounce) bag frozen mashed potatoes
½ cup milk
3 tablespoons butter, divided
¾ teaspoon salt, divided
12 ounces pork loin, cut into ½-inch pieces
½ teaspoon freshly ground black pepper
1 medium onion, diced
1 (6 ounce) microwavable bag peeled baby carrots
1 tablespoon tomato paste
⅓ cup dry red wine
2 tablespoons all-purpose flour
2 cups beef broth
1 cup frozen green peas
1 tablespoon summer savory
½ teaspoon marjoram
½ teaspoon rosemary

Directions
1. Preheat the broiler to high.
2. Microwave the potatoes according to the package directions. Stir in the milk, 2 tablespoons of butter, and ¼ teaspoon salt.
3. While the potatoes cook, heat a Dutch oven over medium-high heat. Add the remaining butter to the pan; swirl to coat. Sprinkle the pork evenly with the remaining salt, and season with pepper.
4. Sauté the pork for 6 minutes, turning to brown on all sides, and remove it from the pot.
5. Add the onion and sauté for 4 minutes, stirring occasionally.
6. While the onion cooks, microwave the carrots on HIGH for 1 ½ minutes.
7. Remove the carrots from the bag and slice them into ½-inch pieces.

8. Stir the tomato paste into the onions and cook for 1 minute, stirring frequently. Deglaze the pot with the wine.
9. Add the flour and whisk for 1 minute, stirring constantly. Gradually add the broth, stirring constantly.
10. Stir in the sliced carrots, peas, and herbs. Bring it to a boil and cook 4 minutes or until slightly thick, stirring occasionally. Remove from the heat and stir in the browned pork.
11. Spoon the mixture into a 2-quart broiler-safe ceramic casserole dish, and top with the mashed potato mixture. Broil 4 minutes or until lightly browned on top.

Nutrition (per serving)
Calories 377, Fat 14 g, Carbs 40 g, Protein 20 g, Sodium 536 mg

Succotash with Crunchy Bacon Topping

Serves: 6 - Prep. time: 10 minutes - Cooking time: 40 minutes

Ingredients
2 cups frozen baby lima beans
6 slices bacon
1 small onion, diced
½ red bell pepper, diced
½ teaspoon salt, divided
2 cloves garlic, minced
2 cups frozen corn kernels, thawed
3 tablespoons all-purpose flour
1 ⅓ cups milk, divided
¼ teaspoon black pepper
¾ cup sharp cheddar cheese, shredded
15 round buttery crackers, coarsely crushed

Directions
1. Preheat the oven to 375°F and grease an 8x8" casserole dish with cooking spray.
2. Cook the lima beans in boiling water for 5 minutes or until crisp-tender; drain.
3. Cook the bacon in a large non-stick skillet over medium heat until crisp. Remove it from the pan, reserving 2 teaspoons of drippings in pan. Crumble the bacon and set aside.
4. Add the onion, bell pepper, ¼ teaspoon of salt, and garlic to the drippings in the pan. Cook for 4 minutes or until tender, stirring frequently. Stir in the lima beans and corn.
5. Place the flour in a small bowl and gradually add ⅓ cup milk, whisking to form a slurry.
6. Add the slurry, the remaining salt, remaining milk, and black pepper to the corn mixture. Cook over medium heat for 3 minutes or until thick and bubbly. Remove it from the heat.

7. Add the cheese and stir until it melts. Spoon the mixture into the baking dish.
8. Sprinkle the cracker crumbs and bacon on top of the casserole. Bake for 20 minutes or until lightly browned on top and bubbly around the edges.

Nutrition (per serving)
Calories 258, Fat 8 g, Carbs 34 g, Protein 13 g, Sodium 514 mg

Creamy Sausage Pie

Serves: 12 - Prep. time: 20 minutes - Cooking time: 1 hour

Ingredients
1 pound breakfast sausage, casings removed
3 cups shredded potatoes, drained and pressed
¼ cup butter, melted
1 cup cheddar cheese, shredded
1 small onion, shredded
1 (16 ounce) container small curd cottage cheese
6 large eggs
1 cup spinach, finely sliced

Directions
1. Preheat the oven to 375°F. Lightly grease a 9x13" baking dish.
2. Place the sausage in a large, deep skillet. Cook over medium-high heat until evenly brown. Drain, crumble, and set aside.
3. In the prepared baking dish, stir together the shredded potatoes and butter. Line the bottom and sides of the baking dish with the mixture. In a bowl, mix the sausage, cheddar cheese, onion, cottage cheese, eggs, and spinach.
4. Pour the sausage mixture over the potato mixture.
5. Bake 1 hour, or until a toothpick inserted into center of the casserole comes out clean. Let it cool for 5 minutes before serving.

Nutrition (per serving)
Calories 355, Fat 26 g, Carbs 8 g, Protein 22 g, Sodium 755 mg

Sausage and Caramelized Onion Bread Pudding

Serves: 4 - Prep. time: 15 minutes - Cooking time: 1 hour

Ingredients
1 ⅓ cups milk
¼ teaspoon dry mustard
⅛ teaspoon salt
2 large eggs
1 large egg white
8 slices day-old French bread, cut in 1-inch cubes
2 tablespoons unsalted butter
2 large yellow onions, diced
1 teaspoon rubbed sage
Salt and pepper to taste
¼ cup apple juice
4 ounces Italian sausage, casings removed
¾ cup sharp cheddar cheese, shredded, divided

Directions
1. Combine the milk, mustard, salt, eggs, and egg white in a large bowl and whisk well. Add the bread cubes and toss gently to coat. Let the bread mixture stand 20 minutes.
2. Preheat the oven to 350°F.
3. Heat a large non-stick skillet over medium heat. Coat the pan with cooking spray. Cook the onions for 10 minutes, stirring occasionally. Add the juice and cook for 5 more minutes, stirring occasionally. Season with sage, salt, and pepper.
4. Meanwhile, crumble the sausage into a separate pan. Cook 10 minutes, or until browned, stirring frequently. Drain the grease, remove it from the heat, and let it stand 5 minutes.
5. Combine the sausage mixture and the onions with the bread mixture; stir well to combine. Fold in the cheese.
6. Spoon into the baking dish, and bake for 40 minutes, or until set and lightly browned. Let stand for 10 minutes before serving.

Nutrition (per serving)
Calories 481, Fat 22 g, Carbs 46 g, Protein 27 g, Sodium 897 mg

Overnight Bacon, Gruyère and Ham Strata

Serves: 6 - Prep. time: 15 minutes - Cooking time: 35 minutes

Ingredients
2 cups milk
1 cup scallions, chopped
4 eggs, lightly beaten
1 tablespoon Dijon mustard
¼ teaspoon cayenne pepper
10 cups sourdough bread, cut into ½-inch cubes toasted
¼ cup ham, diced
1 cup Gruyère cheese, shredded
4 bacon slices, cooked and crumbled

Directions
1. Combine the milk, scallions, eggs, mustard, and pepper in a large bowl, stirring with a whisk. Add the bread cubes and ham; stir well to combine.
2. Spray a 2-quart baking pan with cooking spray. Pour the mixture in, and sprinkle with shredded cheese. Cover, and chill 8 hours or overnight.
3. Preheat the oven to 350°F.
4. Uncover the dish and bake for 20 minutes. Sprinkle with bacon. Bake an additional 15 minutes or until the bread mixture is set and the cheese is melted.

Nutrition (per serving)
Calories 355, Fat 14 g, Carbs 3 g, Protein 22 g, Sodium 849 mg

Vegetarian

Wild Rice and Kale Bake

Serves: 6 - Prep. time: 25 minutes - Cooking time: 25 minutes

Ingredients
2 large bunches of kale, torn
1 cup water
1 pound mushrooms, sliced
3 tablespoons olive oil, divided
2 cloves garlic, minced
2 tablespoons fresh tarragon, chopped
¼ teaspoon nutmeg
Salt and pepper to taste
4 tablespoons all-purpose flour
1 cup milk
1 cup vegetable broth
¼ cup heavy cream
4 cups cooked wild rice
1 ½ cups gruyere cheese, shredded

Directions
1. Grease a 3-quart casserole dish and set it aside. Preheat the oven to 375°F.
2. Heat a very large skillet over medium-high heat. Add the kale to the skillet, together with the water. Cover, and cook for 10–15 minutes, stirring occasionally, until the kale is wilted.
3. Remove the softened kale from the skillet, drain any excess water, and set it aside.
4. Return the skillet to medium heat and add 3 tablespoons of olive oil. Brown the mushrooms and season them with salt and pepper. Add the garlic, tarragon and nutmeg, and cook for about 1 minute. Stir in the kale and mix well.
5. Sprinkle the flour over the kale and mushrooms and cook for 1 minute.

6. Add the milk and broth, bring it to a boil, and cook 2–3 minutes, or until the sauce thickens. Add the cream and stir to combine. Remove the pan from the heat and stir in the cooked wild rice. Pour the mixture into the prepared casserole dish.
7. Sprinkle the cheese over the casserole. Bake for 20–25 minutes, or until the cheese is melted. Serve!

Nutrition (per serving)
Calories 330, Fat 16 g, Carbs 48 g, Protein 17 g, Sodium 480 mg

Tangy Spinach and Cheese Pasta

Serves: 6 - Prep. time: 30 minutes - Cooking time: 50 minutes

Ingredients
10 ounces dry rotini pasta
1 (5 ounce) package fresh baby spinach
1 tablespoon olive oil
2 large onions, diced
¼ cup all-purpose flour
3 cloves garlic, minced
2 ½ cups milk
½ cup dry white wine
1 cup Parmesan cheese, grated, divided
1 teaspoon salt
½ teaspoon black pepper
½ teaspoon grated lemon rind
¾ cup buttery round crackers, crushed

Directions
1. Preheat the oven to 350°F and coat a 9x13" baking dish with cooking spray.
2. Cook the pasta in boiling water for 8 minutes, or until it is almost done. Remove it from the heat and stir in the spinach. Let it stand for 2 minutes, or until the spinach wilts. Drain well.
3. Meanwhile, heat a large non-stick skillet over medium heat and add the olive oil and onions. Cook for 15 minutes or until golden brown, stirring frequently.
4. Add the flour and garlic and cook 1 minute, stirring constantly with a whisk. Gradually stir in the milk and wine, and cook until the sauce boils and thickens, stirring constantly (about 10 minutes).
5. Stir in three-quarters of the cheese, salt, pepper, and lemon rind.
6. Remove the pot from the heat. Add pasta mixture to the onion mixture and toss gently to coat.

7. Spoon the pasta mixture into the baking dish. Sprinkle half the cracker crumbs over the pasta, and top evenly with the remaining quarter cup cheese. Top with the last of the cracker crumbs.
8. Bake for 50 minutes, or until browned and bubbly.

Nutrition (per serving)
Calories 399, Fat 10 g, Carbs 63 g, Protein 18 g, Sodium 611 mg

Butternut Squash Lasagna

Serves: 6 - Prep. time: 45 minutes - Cooking time: 1 hour

Ingredients
1 tablespoon olive oil
2 cups chopped onion
10 cups baby spinach
¾ cup sharp provolone cheese, shredded
½ cup chopped fresh flat-leaf parsley
1 teaspoon salt
½ teaspoon black pepper
1 teaspoon oregano
2 large eggs
2 (15 ounce) containers 2% cottage cheese
3 cups butternut squash, peeled and diced
6 cups marinara or pasta sauce
12 oven-ready lasagna noodles (no boiling)
1 cup fresh Parmesan cheese, grated

Directions
1. Preheat the oven to 375°F. Coat the bottom and sides of two 8x8" baking dishes with cooking spray.
2. Heat a large Dutch oven over medium-high heat. Add the oil and onion; sauté 4 minutes or until tender.
3. Add the spinach and stir until the spinach wilts. Remove the pot from the heat.
4. Combine the provolone, parsley, salt, pepper, oregano, eggs, and cottage cheese in a large bowl.
5. Place the squash in a microwave-safe bowl. Cover and cook on high for 5 minutes, or until tender.
6. Do the following steps in each baking dish: Spread half a cup of marinara or pasta sauce in the bottom of the dish. Arrange 2 noodles over the sauce and spread 1 cup cheese mixture over the noodles. Arrange 1 ½ cups of squash cubes over the cheese mixture, and ¾ cup of sauce over the squash.

7. Arrange 2 noodles over the sauce and spread 1 cup of cheese mixture over the noodles. Spoon 1 ½ cups of the onion mixture over the cheese mixture and spread ¾ cup of sauce over that.
8. Arrange 2 noodles over the sauce, spread 1 cup of marinara evenly over the noodles. Sprinkle with ½ cup of Parmesan.
9. Cover each pan with foil. Bake for 30 minutes, and then uncover and bake an additional 30 minutes.

To freeze unbaked lasagna: Prepare through step 8. Cover with plastic wrap, pressing to remove as much air as possible. Wrap with heavy-duty foil. Store in the freezer for up to 2 months.

To prepare frozen unbaked lasagna: Thaw completely in the refrigerator (about 24 hours). Preheat the oven to 375°F. Remove the foil and set it aside. Discard the plastic wrap. Cover the lasagna with the reserved foil; bake at 375° for 1 hour. Uncover and bake an additional 30 minutes or until bubbly.

Nutrition (per serving)
Calories 289, Fat 13 g, Carbs 28 g, Protein 19 g, Sodium 560 mg

Eggplant Parmesan

Serves: 10 - Prep. time: 30 min - Cooking time: 1 h, 15 min

Ingredients
2 large eggs, lightly beaten
1 tablespoon water
2 cups panko breadcrumbs
¼ cup Parmigiano-Reggiano cheese, grated
2 (1 pound) eggplants, peeled and cut crosswise into ½-inch slices

Filling:
½ cup fresh basil, chopped
¼ cup Parmigiano-Reggiano cheese, grated
½ teaspoon crushed red pepper
3 cloves garlic, minced
1 teaspoon onion powder
Salt and pepper to taste
2 (8 ounce) containers 2% cottage cheese
1 large egg, lightly beaten

Remaining ingredients:
4 cups pasta sauce
1 ½ cups mozzarella cheese, shredded

Directions
1. Preheat the oven to 375°F and prepare a 9x13" baking dish and 2 cookie sheets with cooking spray.
2. Prepare the eggplant. Combine the eggs and 1 tablespoon of water in a shallow dish. Combine the panko and ¼ cup Parmigiano-Reggiano in a second shallow dish.
3. Dip each slice of eggplant in the egg mixture, and then dredge it in the panko mixture, pressing gently so the breadcrumbs stick, and shaking off any excess.
4. Place the coated eggplant slices 1 inch apart on the baking sheets. Bake them for 30 minutes or until they are golden, turning them once and rotating the baking sheets after 15 minutes.

5. To make the filling, combine the basil, ¼ cup Parmigiano-Reggiano cheese, garlic, onion powder, salt, pepper, cottage cheese, and egg.
6. To assemble, spoon ½ cup of pasta sauce into the baking dish. Layer half the eggplant slices over the pasta sauce.
7. Top with about ¾ cup pasta sauce and spread half of the cottage cheese mixture over sauce. Follow with a third of the mozzarella. Repeat the layers once, ending with about 1 cup of pasta sauce.
8. Cover tightly with aluminum foil coated with cooking spray. Bake at 375° for 35 minutes. Remove the foil and top with the remaining third of the mozzarella. Bake for 10 more minutes, or until the sauce is bubbly and cheese melts; cool 10 minutes before serving.

Nutrition (per serving)
Calories 318, Fat 15 g, Carbs 27 g, Protein 19 g, Sodium 655 mg

Green Bean Casserole

Serves: 6 - Prep. time: 20 minutes - Cooking time: 50 minutes

Ingredients
For the Fried Onions
3 tablespoons cornstarch
3 tablespoons all-purpose flour
½ teaspoon salt
1 medium onion, sliced into thin strips
Vegetable oil for frying

For the Casserole
2 tablespoons olive oil
1 small onion, finely diced
2 cloves garlic, minced
8 ounces white mushrooms, finely sliced
2 cups milk, divided
2 tablespoons cornstarch
1 pound fresh green beans, cleaned, trimmed, and steamed
½ teaspoon summer savory
½ teaspoon celery seed
Salt and pepper, to taste
½ cup Parmesan cheese, grated, divided

Directions
1. For the onions: In a large resealable bag, combine the cornstarch, flour, and salt. Add the onions and shake the bag to combine. Remove the onions from the bag.
2. Fill a large, heavy-bottomed skillet with a quarter inch of vegetable oil. Heat it over medium-high heat until hot and shimmering. When it is hot, shake any excess flour from the onions, and cook them in batches until golden and crispy. Remove them with a slotted spoon and set them aside on paper tower to drain.
3. For the casserole: Preheat the oven to 350°F. In a medium saucepan, heat the olive oil over medium-high heat. Add the diced onion and garlic. Sauté until soft, stirring frequently. Add the mushrooms, and cook until they are soft and tender, stirring frequently, about 2 minutes.

4. Add 1 ¾ cups of milk, together with the thyme and celery seed. Bring it to a boil.
5. Combine the remaining ¼ cup of milk and two tablespoons of cornstarch until smooth. Whisk the slurry into the onion mixture and allow it to come to a boil and thicken, about 1 minute. Season with salt and pepper to taste.
6. Add the green beans to the sauce and stir to combine. Pour the mixture into a 2-quart casserole dish. Top with half the grated Parmesan cheese, and cover with foil. Bake for 30 minutes.
7. Remove the foil. Sprinkle the fried onions and remaining cheese over the top of the casserole. Return it to the oven until it is bubbling and lightly golden brown, about 7 minutes.

Nutrition (per serving)
Calories 143, Fat 8 g, Carbs 18 g, Protein 2 g, Sodium 1051 mg

Spinach Pasta Casserole

Serves: 4 - Prep. time: 20 minutes - Cooking time: 30 minutes

Ingredients
12 ounces spinach pasta
5 ounces fresh baby spinach
2 large shallots, peeled and chopped
3 cloves garlic, minced
2 ounces Feta cheese, crumbled
½ cup low-fat Greek yogurt
½ sour cup cream
½ cup basil pesto
Black pepper to taste
1 large egg

Directions
1. Heat the oven to 350°F and lightly grease an 8x8" baking dish with cooking spray.
2. Bring a large pot of salted water to a boil and add the spinach pasta. Cook according to the package instructions, drain, and set aside.
3. Meanwhile, in a large bowl, combine the chopped spinach, shallots, and garlic. Toss with the Feta cheese.
4. In a separate bowl, whisk together the yogurt, sour cream, and pesto. Add black pepper to taste. Whisk in the egg.
5. Stir the cooked pasta together with the spinach and shallots. Pour in the sauce and toss to coat. Spread in the prepared baking dish or cover it and refrigerate for the next day.
6. Bake for 30 minutes or until browned on top and lightly bubbling.
7. Let it cool for 10 minutes, and then serve.

Nutrition (per serving)
Calories 852, Fat 59 g, Carbs 27 g, Protein 26 g, Sodium 953 mg

Artichoke and Spinach Casserole

Serves: 5–6 - Prep. time: 15 minutes - Cooking time: 35 minutes

Ingredients
2 tablespoons butter
1 small onion, diced
3 garlic cloves, minced
10 ounces frozen spinach, thawed and drained
2 cups marinated artichoke hearts, chopped
Salt and pepper to taste
2 eggs
¾ cup plain Greek yogurt
½ cup mozzarella cheese
¼ cup pepper jack cheese
3 cups quinoa, cooked (1 cup dry quinoa)
¼ cup Parmesan cheese

Directions
1. Preheat the oven to 375°F and prepare a 2-quart casserole dish with cooking spray.
2. Melt the butter over medium heat in a sauté pan, and cook the onion and garlic for a few minutes, until fragrant.
3. Squeeze the excess water out of the spinach and add it to the pan. Add the chopped artichoke hearts and cook for five minutes. Season with salt and pepper.
4. Meanwhile, combine the eggs, yogurt and cheese in a large bowl and mix well.
5. Remove the spinach artichoke mixture from the heat and allow it to cool for a few minutes before adding it to the bowl with the eggs and cheese. Stir in the cooked quinoa as well.
6. Place the mixture into the casserole dish, smoothing the top with the back of a spoon. Sprinkle the Parmesan cheese on top and cook for 30–35 minutes, until the top is light golden brown. Serve warm and enjoy!

Nutrition (per serving)
Calories 357, Fat 14 g, Carbs 34 g, Protein 27 g, Sodium 479 mg

Savory Mushroom Bread Pudding

Serves: 8 - Prep. time: 10 minutes - Cooking time: 45 minutes

Ingredients
7 cups cubed sourdough bread (1-inch cubes)
1 ½ cups milk
½ cup heavy cream
1 small celery root (about 12 ounces), peeled and cut into ½-inch pieces (about 2 cups)
Salt and pepper to taste
½ teaspoon paprika
½ teaspoon onion powder
2 tablespoons butter
1 pound mushrooms, such as shiitake, maitake, cremini, and oyster, thinly sliced
1 clove garlic, minced
¼ cup white wine
2 large eggs, lightly beaten
1 tablespoon fresh thyme leaves, plus sprigs for garnish
½ cup crumbled Feta

Directions
1. Preheat the oven to 400°F and coat a 2-quart baking dish and a cookie sheet with cooking spray.
2. Arrange the bread cubes on the tray, and toast them until golden, about 10 minutes. (Be careful they don't burn.)
3. Meanwhile, combine the milk, cream, and celery root in a small saucepan. Bring it to a boil, then reduce the heat and simmer until the celery root is tender, about 10 minutes. Let it cool slightly.
4. Transfer the mixture to a blender and purée until smooth. Season with salt, pepper, paprika, and onion powder.
5. In a large skillet, melt the butter over medium-high heat. Add the mushrooms and cook, stirring occasionally, until they have released most of their moisture and become golden, about 9 minutes. Add the garlic and stir for one minute.

6. Add the wine and stir, scraping up any browned bits with a wooden spoon. Season with salt and pepper and transfer the mixture to a bowl.
7. In a large bowl, whisk together the celery root mixture, eggs, and thyme leaves. Fold in the toasted bread and mushrooms. Transfer the casserole to the prepared dish, and sprinkle with cheese. Garnish with thyme sprigs and bake until the custard is set and the top is lightly browned, about 25 minutes. Let it cool slightly before serving.

Nutrition (per serving)
Calories 282, Fat 14 g, Carbs 23 g, Protein 18 g, Sodium 633 mg

Mashed Potato Bake

Serves: 8 - Prep. time: 15 minutes - Cooking time: 40 minutes

Ingredients
3 pounds Yukon gold potatoes, peeled and chopped
3 cloves garlic, crushed and chopped
2 teaspoons salt, divided
½ teaspoon black pepper
6 ounces cream cheese, softened
½ cup Parmesan cheese, grated
½ cup breadcrumbs
2 tablespoons chives, minced

Directions
1. Preheat the oven to 350°F and coat a 9x9" baking pan with cooking spray.
2. Place the potatoes, garlic, and ½ teaspoon of salt in a large saucepan, and cover with water. Bring it to a boil. Reduce the heat and simmer 15 minutes, or until tender. Drain in a colander over a bowl, reserving ½ cup of cooking liquid.
3. Press the potato pieces (and garlic) through a ricer into a large bowl. Stir in the reserved cooking liquid, the remaining 1 ½ teaspoons of salt, pepper, and cream cheese.
4. Spoon the potato mixture into the baking dish. Bake for 20 minutes or until thoroughly heated.
5. Preheat the broiler.
6. Combine the Parmesan and bread crumbs and sprinkle them evenly over the potatoes. Broil 4 minutes, or until golden brown. Sprinkle with chives.

Nutrition (per serving)
Calories 243, Fat 7 g, Carbs 38 g, Protein 8 g, Sodium 361 mg

Traditional Sweet Potato Casserole

Serves: 16 - Prep. time: 30 minutes - Cooking time: 25 minutes

Ingredients
2 ½ pounds sweet potatoes, peeled and cut in 1-inch cubes
¾ cup packed brown sugar
¼ cup butter, softened
1 ½ teaspoons salt
1 teaspoon vanilla extract
½ cup finely chopped pecans, divided
2 cups white miniature marshmallows

Directions
1. Preheat the oven to 375°F and coat a 7x11" casserole dish with cooking spray.
2. Place the sweet potatoes in a Dutch oven and cover them with cold water. Bring them to a boil, reduce the heat, and simmer for 15 minutes or until very tender. Drain, and cool slightly.
3. Place the potatoes in a large bowl. Add the sugar, butter, salt, and vanilla
4. Mash the sweet potato mixture with a potato masher, and fold in ¼ cup of pecans. Scrape the mixture in an even layer in the casserole dish.
5. Sprinkle with the remaining ¼ cup pecans and top with marshmallows.
6. Bake for 25 minutes, or until golden.

Nutrition (per serving)
Calories 186, Fat 6 g, Carbs 33 g, Protein 2 g, Sodium 272 mg

Desserts

Bakery French Toast

Serves: 4–5 - Prep. time: 15 minutes - Cooking time: 50 minutes

Ingredients
1 loaf day-old bakery cinnamon-raisin bread (14 slices)
3 eggs, lightly beaten
1 ½ cups half & half
1 cup whipping cream
½ cup brown sugar
½ teaspoon vanilla extract
½ teaspoon ground cinnamon
Maple syrup, for serving

Directions
1. Preheat the oven to 375°F. Grease an 8x8" baking pan with cooking spray.
2. Line the bottom of the baking pan with 3 slices of bread, cut to fit. Top with 3 more slices, cut to fit. Place 8 slices across the top in 2 rows; shingle-fashion. Press down firmly.
3. Whisk the eggs in a medium bowl. Mix in the half & half, cream, sugar, vanilla, and cinnamon. Pour the egg mixture evenly over the bread and cover tightly with foil.
4. Bake for 40 minutes. Remove the foil and bake 10 minutes longer. Let stand 10 minutes before serving. Serve with maple syrup.

Nutrition (per serving)
Calories 398, Fat 16 g, Carbs 54 g, Protein 10 g, Sodium 369 mg

Apricot Apple Crisp

Serves: 10 - Prep. time: 15 minutes - Cooking time: 30 minutes

Ingredients
1 teaspoon butter, for greasing
5 Granny Smith apples, sliced
1 cup dried apricots, finely chopped
1 tablespoon lemon juice
⅓ cup brown sugar
½ cup all-purpose flour

Topping:
¾ cup rolled oats
¾ cup brown sugar
½ teaspoon salt
½ teaspoon nutmeg
1 teaspoon cinnamon
Tiny pinch cloves
½ cup cold butter, cubed

Directions
1. Preheat the oven to 375°F and grease an 8x8" baking dish with butter.
2. In a bowl, mix the apple slices, cranberries, lemon juice, and sugar. Pour the mixture into the baking dish.
3. In a separate bowl, make the topping by mixing the oats, flour, sugar, salt, nutmeg, cinnamon, and cloves. Blend in the butter using a pastry cutter.
4. Sprinkle the topping over the apples.
5. Bake for 30 minutes, until the topping is brown and crisp.
6. Serve warm with ice cream or whipped cream.

Nutrition (per serving)
Calories 368, Fat 12 g, Carbs 66 g, Protein 3 g, Sodium 269 mg

Pineapple Casserole Dessert

Serves: 4–6 - Prep. time: 15 minutes - Cooking time: 65 minutes

Ingredients
1 cup butter
1 ½ cups white sugar
6 eggs
1 (15-ounce) can crushed pineapple, drained
9 slices bread, cubed
¼ cup sharp cheddar cheese, shredded

Directions
1. Preheat the oven to 325°F.
2. Cream the butter and sugar together. Beat in the eggs, one at a time, until fully incorporated. Fold in the pineapple and bread.
3. Pour the mixture into a 9x13" baking dish.
4. Bake for 1 hour, until the center springs back when touched lightly.
5. Sprinkle the cheese evenly over the top, and return to the oven to melt the cheese, 2–5 minutes.

Nutrition (per serving)
Calories 284, Fat 11 g, Carbs 43 g, Protein 4 g, Sodium 243 mg

Lemon Poke Cake

Serves: 12 - Prep. time: 20 minutes - Refrigeration time: 4–8 hours

Ingredients
1 boxed lemon cake, baked in a 9x13" pan and cooled
2 cups cooked lemon pudding, not yet set (reserve ¼ cup for drizzling)
1 (8 ounce) container whipped dessert topping
½ cup white chocolate chips
½ cup chopped pecans

Directions
1. Use the handle of a wooden spoon to poke holes evenly throughout the baked cake (approximately 20–25 holes).
2. Pour the lemon pudding over the cake, filling the holes. Use a rubber spatula to spread it evenly over the cake.
3. Spread the whipped topping over top. Sprinkle on the white chips and pecans. Drizzle with remaining lemon pudding.
4. Let it chill for at least 4 hours. Overnight is best.

Nutrition (per serving)
Calories 301, Carbs 44 g, Fat 12 g, Protein 3 g, Sodium 309 mg

Raspberry Cobbler

Serves: 8 - Prep. time: 15 minutes - Cooking time: 30 minutes

Ingredients
1 cup all-purpose flour
1 ½ cups white sugar, divided
1 teaspoon baking powder
½ teaspoon salt
6 tablespoons cold butter
¼ cup boiling water
2 tablespoons cornstarch
¼ cup cold water
1 tablespoon lemon juice
4 cups fresh raspberries, rinsed and drained
1 tablespoon vanilla

Directions
1. Preheat the oven to 400°F. Line a baking sheet with aluminum foil.
2. In a large bowl, mix the flour, ½ cup sugar, baking powder, and salt. Cut in the butter until the mixture resembles coarse crumbs.
3. Stir in ¼ cup boiling water, just until the mixture is evenly moist.
4. In a separate bowl, dissolve the cornstarch in the cold water. Mix in the remaining 1 cup sugar, lemon juice, and raspberries.
5. Transfer the mixture to a cast iron skillet, and bring it to a boil, stirring frequently. Remove it from the heat and stir in the vanilla.
6. Drop the batter into the skillet by spoonfuls.
7. Place the skillet on the foil-lined baking sheet and bake for 25 minutes, until the dough is golden brown.

Nutrition (per serving)
Calories 318, Fat 9 g, Carbs 58 g, Protein 3 g, Sodium 253 mg

Georgia Cobbler

Serves: 8–10 - Prep. time: 40 minutes - Cooking time: 40 minutes

Ingredients
16 cups fresh peaches, peeled and diced
3 cups sugar
⅓ cup all-purpose flour
½ teaspoon cinnamon
¼ teaspoon allspice
1 ½ teaspoons vanilla
⅔ cup butter
2 packages refrigerated pie dough
½ cup chopped pecans, toasted
¼ cup sugar
Vanilla ice cream, for serving

Directions
1. Combine the peaches, sugar, flour, cinnamon, and allspice in a Dutch oven, and let it sit until the sugar dissolves.
2. Set it over medium-high heat and bring it to a boil. Reduce the heat to low, and simmer 10 minutes or until tender.
3. Remove it from the heat. Add the vanilla and butter, stirring until the butter melts.
4. Preheat the oven to 475°F and coat a 9x13" baking dish with cooking spray.
5. Unfold 2 pie crusts. Sprinkle ¼ cup of pecans and 2 tablespoons sugar evenly over 1 pie crust and top it with other pie crust. Roll it our to a 12-inch circle, gently pressing pecans into pastry. Cut into 1 ½-inch strips.
6. Repeat with remaining pie crusts, pecans, and sugar.
7. Spoon half of the peach mixture into the baking dish. Arrange half of pastry strips in a lattice design over the peach mixture.
8. Bake for 20–25 minutes, or until lightly browned.
9. Spoon the remaining peach mixture over the baked pastry. Top with remaining the pastry strips in a lattice design. Bake 15–18 more minutes.
10. Serve warm or cold with vanilla ice cream.

Nutrition (per serving)
Calories 374, Fat 14 g, Carbs 59 g, Protein 4 g, Sodium 182 mg

Overnight Praline Pumpkin Pudding

Serves: 11 - Prep. time: 15 minutes plus 8–24 hours chilling - Cooking time: 1 hour

Ingredients
Bread pudding:
4 large eggs
2 (15 ounce) cans pumpkin purée
1 ½ cups milk
¾ cup half & half
1 cup white sugar
1 teaspoon ground cinnamon
½ teaspoon salt
½ teaspoon ground nutmeg
Pinch ground cardamom
1 teaspoon vanilla extract
1 loaf French bread, cut into 1-inch pieces (about 10 cups)

Caramel-pecan sauce:
1 cup pecans, chopped
1 cup firmly packed light brown sugar
½ cup butter
3 tablespoons light corn syrup
1 teaspoon vanilla extract

Directions
1. Prepare the bread puddings: Whisk together the eggs, pumpkin, milk, half & half, sugar, cinnamon, salt, nutmeg, cardamom, and vanilla until well blended.
2. Add the bread pieces, stirring to thoroughly coat. Cover with plastic wrap, and chill for 8–24 hours.
3. Preheat the oven to 350°F. Spoon the bread mixture into eleven 6-ounce lightly greased ramekins. (The ramekins will be completely full, and the mixture will mound slightly.)
4. Bake for 50 minutes, shielding with foil after 30 minutes.

5. During the last 15 minutes of baking, prepare the caramel-pecan sauce. Heat the pecans in a medium skillet over medium-low heat, stirring often, for 3–5 minutes or until lightly toasted and fragrant.
6. Cook the brown sugar, butter, and corn syrup in a small saucepan over medium heat, stirring occasionally for 3–4 minutes, or until the sugar is dissolved. Remove it from the heat and stir in the vanilla and pecans.
7. Remove the bread puddings from the oven and drizzle with caramel-pecan sauce. Bake 5 minutes, or until the sauce is thoroughly heated and begins to bubble.

Nutrition (per serving)
Calories 356, Fat 24 g, Carbs 29 g, Protein 5 g, Sodium 162 mg

Tipsy Baked Winter Fruit

Serves: 6–8 - Prep. time: 15 minutes plus up to 24 hours chill time - Cooking time: 50 minutes

Ingredients
10 ounces dried figs, trimmed and halved
7 ounces dried apricots
5 ounces dried apples
2 cups apple cider
⅔ cup dry sherry
½ cup golden raisins
2 navel oranges, peeled and sectioned
1 (3-inch) cinnamon stick Brown

Optional: Whipped cream, for serving

Directions
1. Place all the ingredients EXCEPT the orange slices for garnishing in a 7x11" baking dish, and gently toss to combine. Cover with aluminum foil, and chill for 12–24 hours.
2. Preheat the oven to 350°F. Bake the fruit mixture, covered, for 45–50 minutes or until it is thoroughly heated, and the fruit is soft.
3. Let it stand, covered, for 15 minutes. Remove and discard the cinnamon stick. Serve with whipped cream, if desired.

Nutrition (per serving)
Calories 496, Fat 8 g, Carbs 104 g, Protein 2 g, Sodium 90 mg

Recipe Index

Breakfast 7
   Mushroom Hash Brown Morning Casserole 7
   Pumpkin Spice Latte Quinoa Breakfast Casserole 9
   Berry Cream Cheese French Toast Casserole 11
   Gobble Gobble Spinach and Mushroom Egg Bake 12
   Roasted Broccoli and Ham Breakfast Casserole 13
   Overnight Sausage and Spiced Apple Breakfast Casserole 14
   Overnight Sweet and Savory Breakfast Casserole 15
   Overnight Pumpkin French Toast 16

Chicken and Turkey 17
   Chicken Tetrazzini 17
   Chicken Tamale Casserole 19
   Mom's Creamy Chicken and Broccoli Casserole 20
   King Ranch Chicken and Quinoa Casserole 21
   Baked Chicken and Sweet Potato Enchilada 23
   Creamy Chicken Quinoa and Broccoli Casserole 25
   Turkey Taco Mexican Lasagna 27
   Healthy Broccoli Chicken Casserole 29
   Tex-Mex Casserole 30
   Chicken Mushroom and Potato Bake 31
   Enchiladas Supreme 33
   Turkey Sausage Potato Bake 35
   Dreamy Creamy Enchiladas 36
   Zucchini Chicken Bake 37
   Easy Tex-Mex Chicken 38
   Southern Chicken and Biscuit Bake 39

Beef 41
   Quick Pastitsio 41
   Unstuffed Cabbage Casserole 43
   Superfood Taco Casserole 44
   Beefy Tots Casserole 45
   Spaghetti Squash Beef and Bubble 46
   Easy Beef Casserole 47
   Ravioli Twist 48
   Beef Stew Bake 49
   Beef Goulash 50

Pork	51
Bacon with Roasted Butternut Squash Pasta	51
Broccoli Sausage Quinoa Casserole	53
Creamy Cauliflower with Bacon	55
Pork and Cabbage	56
Quick Shepherd's Pie	57
Succotash with Crunchy Bacon Topping	59
Creamy Sausage Pie	61
Sausage and Caramelized Onion Bread Pudding	62
Overnight Bacon, Gruyère and Ham Strata	63
Vegetarian	65
Wild Rice and Kale Bake	65
Tangy Spinach and Cheese Pasta	67
Butternut Squash Lasagna	69
Eggplant Parmesan	71
Green Bean Casserole	73
Spinach Pasta Casserole	75
Artichoke and Spinach Casserole	76
Savory Mushroom Bread Pudding	77
Mashed Potato Bake	79
Traditional Sweet Potato Casserole	80
Desserts	81
Bakery French Toast	81
Apricot Apple Crisp	82
Pineapple Casserole Dessert	83
Lemon Poke Cake	84
Raspberry Cobbler	85
Georgia Cobbler	86
Overnight Praline Pumpkin Pudding	87
Tipsy Baked Winter Fruit	89

Also by Louise Davidson

Soulful
SOUTHERN
COOKING
FAVORITE SOUTHERN COMFORT FOOD RECIPES
Louise Davidson

SLOW COOKER
SOUP
Cookbook
Easy Crock Pot Soup Meal Recipes
Louise Davidson

FIX, COOK & SERVE
LOW CARB
SLOW COOKER
One-Pot Meals
Convenient 8-Hour +
Crock Pot Recipes
LOUISE DAVIDSON

Fix, Cook, & Serve!
Slow Cooker
COOKBOOK
Easy One-Pot Meal
Crock Pot Recipes
LOUISE DAVIDSON

HOMEMADE MEALS
FAST
QUICK AND EASY
PRESSURE COOKER
Recipes
Louise Davidson

Freezer Meals
Recipes
EASY ONE-POT MAKE AHEAD
DUMP MEALS
LOUISE DAVIDSON

DUTCH OVEN
COOKING
EASY ONE-POT MEAL RECIPES
LOUISE DAVIDSON

Louise Davidson
AUNT GERTRUDE'S SECRET PIE
Cookbook
Sweet and Savory Pie Recipes

Fermentation
For Beginners
EASY RECIPES FOR
Louise Davidson

Appendix
Cooking Conversion Charts

1. Measuring Equivalent Chart

Type	Imperial	Imperial	Metric
Weight	1 dry ounce		28g
	1 pound	16 dry ounces	0.45 kg
Volume	1 teaspoon		5 ml
	1 dessert spoon	2 teaspoons	10 ml
	1 tablespoon	3 teaspoons	15 ml
	1 Australian tablespoon	4 teaspoons	20 ml
	1 fluid ounce	2 tablespoons	30 ml
	1 cup	16 tablespoons	240 ml
	1 cup	8 fluid ounces	240 ml
	1 pint	2 cups	470 ml
	1 quart	2 pints	0.95 l
	1 gallon	4 quarts	3.8 l
Length	1 inch		2.54 cm

* Numbers are rounded to the closest equivalent

2. Oven Temperature Equivalent Chart

Fahrenheit (°F)	Celsius (°C)	Gas Mark
220	100	
225	110	1/4
250	120	1/2
275	140	1
300	150	2
325	160	3
350	180	4
375	190	5
400	200	6
425	220	7
450	230	8
475	250	9
500	260	

* Celsius (°C) = T (°F)-32] * 5/9
** Fahrenheit (°F) = T (°C) * 9/5 + 32
*** Numbers are rounded to the closest equivalent

Made in the USA
Columbia, SC
15 January 2020